REFERENCE GUIDES IN LITERATURE

Ronald Gottesman, *Editor*

Charles W. Chesnutt:
A Reference Guide

Curtis W. Ellison
E. W. Metcalf, Jr.

G. K. HALL & CO., 70 LINCOLN STREET, BOSTON, MASS.

Copyright©1977 by Curtis W. Ellison and E. W. Metcalf, Jr.

Library of Congress Cataloging in Publication Data
Ellison, Curtis W
    Charles W. Chesnutt : a reference guide.

    (Reference guides in literature)
    Bibliography: p.
    Includes index.
    1.   Chesnutt, Charles Waddell, 1858-1932--
Bibliography.   I.   Metcalf, E. W., joint author.
Z8166.2.E44 [PS1292.C6]   016.813'4   77-335
ISBN 0-8161-7825-9

This publication is printed on permanent/durable acid-free paper
MANUFACTURED IN THE UNITED STATES OF AMERICA

For

Lynn and Barbara

Evelyn, Karin, and Justin

Contents

Introduction

Charles Waddell Chesnutt is a significant figure of late nineteenth and early twentieth century American culture. Author of two collections of short stories, many articles, a major biography, three novels, and several unpublished works, Chesnutt became the first black American writer to produce a substantial volume of quality fiction. He was also a successful lawyer, educator, professional stenographer, and often prominent figure in the struggle for racial and social justice. So notable were his accomplishments that in 1928 he received the Spingarn Medal from the National Association for the Advancement of Colored People, an organization he had long supported, for his "pioneer work as a literary artist depicting the life and struggles of Americans of Negro descent, and for his long and useful career as a scholar, worker and freeman" (1928.B2).

This guide to writings about Chesnutt reveals the man in his full dimensions. It shows the reception given his activities and published work during and after his lifetime, to the present. It can be used not only to chart the developing critical reaction to Chesnutt's substantial and important body of fiction, as well as the response to his personal activities, but also the often ominous and confused reaction of American culture to the racial questions which Chesnutt could have avoided but chose not to. For Chesnutt was deeply involved in the issues of his race and day, issues that have not all passed away with the times. Indeed, the reactions to Chesnutt and his work often reveal as much about his critics and their times as about Chesnutt and his.

Chesnutt's Life

Chesnutt was born in a German neighborhood of Cleveland on June 20, 1858. He lived in Cleveland, and in Oberlin, Ohio, for eight years, before moving to Fayetteville, North Carolina, where his father entered the grocery business. In North Carolina, Chesnutt attended a Freedmen's Bureau school and worked in his father's store. But at the age of fourteen, when his father lost his store and his mother died, he was forced to leave school and help support a large family. Offered a job in a saloon, he instead became a "pupil-teacher" in the school where he had been a student, and began an extensive self-education. For several years, Chesnutt worked as a teacher in black schools, read widely in the liberal arts, and focused his education on literature. At the age of twenty-two, he was able to move from assistant to full principal of the state normal school at Fayetteville. Not long after, he married a teacher there, and began a family.

During the next years, Chesnutt devoted considerable attention to educating himself. He sought to master languages and composition, as well as humanities, which he approached with planned reading programs. In his work as a teacher, he sought to inspire his students, and motivate them to emulate his efforts. He tutored in the music and languages of Western culture, and was active in his church. Chesnutt's position was such that in 1880, he was nominated for Fayetteville town commissioner by the Republican party; however, he withdrew from politics because of racial slurs directed against him.

Not long after stifling his political inclinations, Chesnutt deliberately made a somewhat dramatic change in his life: he left North Carolina permanently, and moved to New York City. He worked there as a newspaper columnist until 1883, when he moved to Cleveland. In Cleveland, he first worked in a railroad office, then as a legal stenographer, and, meanwhile, he studied law. He passed the Ohio bar in 1887. And in August of that year, he published a short story, "The Goophered Grapevine," in Atlantic Monthly.

At least since 1882, Chesnutt had tried to publish in magazines and newspapers; in 1885, a short story titled "Uncle Peter's House" appeared in the Cleveland News and Herald. Chesnutt wished to establish himself as a writer, though his legal stenographic service, begun in Cleveland in 1890, brought him considerable financial prosperity and entry into exclusive black social circles before he gained a national literary reputation. Then in 1899, his book of short fiction written in North Carolina black dialect, The Conjure Woman, attracted widespread attention. And in that same year, Chesnutt published both The Wife of His Youth, a second collection of short stories, as well as a biography, Frederick Douglass. He then began to devote his full efforts to writing and lecturing, and thereafter produced prodigiously, with the declared intention of increasing the sensitivity of whites to the humanity of black people through the effect of his writings.

Chesnutt described his effort as a moral crusade that would help "accustom the public mind" to the idea of equality. And he worked at his crusade with extraordinary diligence. Sylvia Lyons Render has stated that between 1885 and 1930, Chesnutt wrote "one play, five poems, six novels, fifty-three essays and speeches, and eighteen short stories," though some are incomplete and several are still unpublished. His stories and tales treat the texture of Afro-American life with considerable sensitivity, while incorporating the overall

theme of racist injustice, often through the use of irony and under-
statement. His three published novels are The House Behind the
Cedars (1900), The Marrow of Tradition (1901), and The Colonel's
Dream (1905). The novels consider themes of race relations more
directly than much of his short fiction.

Chesnutt wrote at a time when the black community did not buy
many novels, and when many American whites were upset by his frank
treatments of racial themes. His novels sold poorly. A declining
interest from publishers accompanied poor sales, and in 1901, he re-
opened his legal stenography firm. After 1905, his productivity as
a writer of fiction declined as sharply as it had risen in 1899,
and thereafter, Chesnutt exerted influence as a prominent private
citizen rather than as a writer. During the period of conflict between Booker T. Washington and W. E. B. DuBois, Chesnutt took a non-
partisan stance, criticizing as well as praising each man from time
to time. He was a member of Washington's Committee of Twelve, as
well as a life-long supporter of the N. A. A. C. P. Throughout the
early twentieth century, he consistently spoke out for black rights,
and took personal action against discriminatory treatment. In 1913,
he was awarded the LL.D. by Wilberforce University, and in 1928,
the Spingarn Medal of the N.A.A.C.P. for distinguished service.

Late in his life, and partly as a consequence of the public
recognition given his social service, Chesnutt's books experienced
a revival and some were re-issued in new editions. His last publication, a retrospective account of his own work, appeared in 1931.
He died in Cleveland, in November of the following year.

Chesnutt's Critical Reputation

Chesnutt's work was first noted substantially in 1898, when his
short story "The Wife of His Youth" was praised as "classic,"
"philosophical," and "delicate." The following year, The Conjure
Woman was widely reviewed. It was described as dealing with "plantation superstitions" that were characteristic of blacks, and reviewed
favorably. Cited as a book of humor and quaint interest that was
notable for its use of black dialect, it was compared to the writings
of Thomas Nelson Page, Paul Laurence Dunbar, and Ruth McEnery Stuart.
Some reviewers mentioned Chesnutt's race, and stated that it made
possible his accurate presentation of blacks. Many reviews of The
Conjure Woman revealed racism, as in the statement that the book was
filled with "the darky belief in the supernatural, the darky mingled
childlikeness and shrewdness." The character of Chesnutt's storyteller, Uncle Julius, attracted the most attention--he was often
said to be cunning, and sometimes charged with selfishness.

The Wife of His Youth received more mixed critical attention.
Many reviewers, not all of them southern, criticized the theme of
miscegenation in the book, and attacked Chesnutt for favoring the

mingling of the races. Some reviewers noted the shift in focus from his first work, but stated that the new book evoked the same "suggestion of reality." On the whole, critical reaction to this second book of short stories was favorable. Both The Wife of His Youth and the biography, Frederick Douglass, were cited at times as examples of the equality of mental ability between blacks and whites. Frederick Douglass was praised for its fidelity to "facts," though an occasional reviewer found the portrait of Douglass too glowing.

By 1900, Chesnutt was being reviewed very widely, and The House Behind the Cedars stimulated some divisions among his reviewers. While many saw Chesnutt's first novel as strengthening his bid for "a secure place in the literary world," some saw it as an attack on racial prejudice, focused on the mulatto's "taint" of "black blood." The theme of the novel was compared to William Dean Howells' "An Imperative Duty," and Howells himself wrote a favorable review of Chesnutt's three books, praising his artistry (1900.B104). Chesnutt's growing reputation was indicated when Booker T. Washington mentioned him in his autobiography (1900.B106).

The Marrow of Tradition greatly exacerbated divisions among Chesnutt's reviewers. Seen as a novel that had strong appeal to "popular sympathies," it was frequently cited as a contemporary Uncle Tom's Cabin that dramatized persecution of blacks for political reasons. As a consequence, Chesnutt was praised highly or excoriated, depending upon the views of his particular critic. Divisions among reviewers did not necessarily follow sectional lines, though Chesnutt had few partisans among whites in the deep south. Throughout 1901 and 1902, The Marrow of Tradition continued to attract wide attention across the United States and in England as well. It was cited as a sectional book, a race book, a political book, and an answer to the novels of Thomas Dixon. Several reviewers, including Howells (1901.B59), asserted that Chesnutt's work was no longer of the same "quality" as his earlier and more "realistic" short stories.

In 1905, with The Colonel's Dream, Chesnutt again elicited quite divergent views. Though reviewers almost universally agreed that this was another "problem" novel of race relations in the south, some classed it with the "lurid" prose of Thomas Dixon, while others found it reserved, quiet, sincere, impressive, and tasteful. Though criticism of Chesnutt again did not fall within sectional lines, many white southern reviewers reacted very defensively to this novel.

The Colonel's Dream continued to attract attention through 1906. After Chesnutt stopped writing new books, however, notices of him diminished considerably in number. And during the remainder of his lifetime, critical attention was sparse, just as it was for all Afro-American writers until perhaps the late 1960's. In 1910, Benjamin Brawley's The Negro in Literature and Art, a pioneer effort at evaluating the literary accomplishments of Afro-Americans, cited

Introduction

Chesnutt as "the foremost novelist and short story writer of the race" (1910.B2). A flurry of attention accompanied Chesnutt's reception of the Spingarn Medal in 1928, and the reprinting of some of his books. In 1931, Vernon Loggins cited Chesnutt as perhaps the best short story writer among Afro-Americans (1931.B1), and in 1933, W. E. B. DuBois called him "the dean of Negro literature" (1933.B3).

With the exception of Hugh Gloster's Negro Voices in American Fiction, where his writings are reviewed and an early effort is made at interpreting them (1948.B4), Chesnutt was the subject of only occasional journal articles and infrequent mentionings in general books, until his biography was published by his daughter in 1952 (1952.A1). In 1953, a vigorous assertion of Chesnutt's superior literary achievement was published in Phylon by Russell Ames (1953.B1), and bibliographical attention was begun at Fisk University in the following year (1954.A1). Throughout the late 1950's and early 1960's, Chesnutt received regular, though infrequent mentionings in general works about Afro-American culture and literature. In 1962, Sylvia Lyons Render completed a doctoral dissertation on Chesnutt (1962.A1), and followed it with several interpretive articles and a major anthology of Chesnutt's short works (1974.B6). A 1968 doctoral dissertation by Charles W. Foster investigated Chesnutt's uses of black dialect (1968.A1).

In the late 1960's, accompanying a considerable increase of interest in black literature and history, some of Chesnutt's books were reprinted with critical introductions by Robert Farnsworth (1969.B3, B4), Sylvia Render (1969.B7), and Darwin Turner (1969.B11). By 1974, at least three more doctoral dissertations had been completed on Chesnutt, and in that year, J. Noel Heermance published Charles W. Chesnutt: America's First Great Black Novelist (1974.B3). Throughout the late 1960's and the 1970's, Chesnutt has continued to receive regular if somewhat incomplete attention, in general works of Afro-American studies, in occasional journal articles, and in bibliographies and anthologies of Afro-American materials. It is fair to state that in the mid-1970's, most literary critics consider him to be the first Afro-American short story artist of considerable merit, and a very important novelist of race relations at the turn of the century.

A Note on Materials Included

This work lists and annotates significant treatments of Chesnutt that appear in biographies, histories, book reviews, introductions to books and to anthologized materials, newspapers, dictionaries, encyclopedias, journal and periodical articles, bibliographies, and historical and critical works about literature. It includes citations of Chesnutt listed in Dissertation Abstracts.

Introduction

Late nineteenth and early twentieth century newspaper reviews are a particularly important source for critical reaction to Chesnutt's writings. Many such mentionings were collected in Chesnutt's scrapbooks, which are held by the Cravath Memorial Library, Fisk University. Newspaper reviews in this collection frequently lack sufficient location data, and only those for which a source and date are available are included here. Page number citations for such reviews are commonly not available. Reviews that are verbatim repetitions of others are not included, and neither are those devoted overwhelmingly to simple plot synopsis.

All citations and annotations are kept as faithful to original sources as possible, both in phrasing and in word use. For example, the word "negro" is used rather than "black" where that wording originally appeared, even though the annotation may be a paraphrase. Outdated spellings have been left intact within quotations. When book titles appearing in newspaper print were not italicized, they have been left this way in direct quotations. In sum, a careful effort has been made to convey the style and tone of the original sources, as well as to present the facts of statements contained within them.

A Note on the Arrangement of Materials

This reference guide presents materials chronologically, by year of publication. Within each year, books devoted entirely or overwhelmingly to Chesnutt are listed first, under section "A." These entries are organized alphabetically by author.

Section "B" for each year lists shorter writings devoted to or mentioning Chesnutt. Many of the early years of Chesnutt material consist largely of newspaper reviews and mentionings for which the authors are not known. All such entries are listed as "Anon.," and organized chronologically by date of publication. Entries of this kind that list only a month of publication and not a more specific date are placed at the beginning of the month's entries. If two anonymously-authored entries have the same date of publication, then the entries are organized alphabetically by title of the review or article. For some untitled items, appropriate titles have been supplied.

A Note on the Index

The index includes the following kinds of items that appear in this reference guide.

> --Names (with the names of fictional characters underscored)
> --Titles of writings by Chesnutt
> --Titles of books and journal articles either wholly about
>   Chesnutt or containing a significant mention of him

Introduction

    --Names of journals and newspapers in which articles about
      Chesnutt appear
    --Selected subject headings

    The index is designed to be used in a number of ways in addition
to the usual ones. During the most active years of Chesnutt's
writing career, most published comments about him and his work appeared in newspapers and journals. Thus the names of these are in-
dexed in order to allow an easy charting of the sources of Chesnutt's
early reputation. In addition, newspaper entries are listed alphabetically by geographical location, making it possible to trace and
compare, geographically, the reactions to Chesnutt and his work.
Finally, the entry for each book, journal, journal article, and newspaper contains when appropriate a subentry to each of Chesnutt's
writings mentioned in that entry. Subentries for journals and newspapers are followed by appropriate numbers to indicate the location
of the discussion of subentries. For books, and periodical articles,
the general entry number is given, followed by a listing of items
discussed within that entry. This allows not only a quick determination of the sources for the reputation of Chesnutt's individual works,
but also a determination of the attitude of an individual source to
Chesnutt's writings as a whole.

Acknowledgments

    Jay Martin of the University of California, Irvine, was instru-
mental in the inception of this project, and gave encouragement along
the way. The following librarians gave special assistance: Ann
Shockley, Beth Howse, and Gregory Engleberg of the Erastus Milo
Cravath Memorial Library, Fisk University; Bill Wortman, Mary Persyn,
and Mary Stanton of the Edgar W. King Library, Miami University; and,
Frank Moorer, Carnegie Library, Wilberforce University. Patrick
Ducey and Marjorie McLellan assisted with research.

Writings about Charles W. Chesnutt, 1887-1975

1887 A BOOKS - NONE

1887 B SHORTER WRITINGS

1　　ANON. "State Capital Gossip." Cleveland Leader (4 March).
　　　　Chesnutt has been admitted to practice law before the
　　Supreme Court. In his study for this he stood at the head
　　of his class by scoring highest on the examination.

1898 A BOOKS - NONE

1898 B SHORTER WRITINGS

1　　ANON. Review of "The Wife of His Youth." Cleveland Recorder
　　　　(7 July).
　　　　　This is one of the best short stories of the year.
　　Chesnutt is a close observer of life, and he can describe
　　what he sees.

2　　ANON. Untitled article. Cleveland Sunday Voice (10 July).
　　　　Tells of recent popularity of two Cleveland writers,
　　Chesnutt and J. Edmund V. Cooke. "The Wife of His Youth"
　　is a "remarkable literary effort."

3　　ANON. Review of "The Wife of His Youth." Cleveland Leader
　　　　(13 July).
　　　　　Style and use of language place Chesnutt in the front
　　rank of short story writers. His use of humor and sarcasm
　　in treating his subject makes him unique.

4　　ANON. "Charles Waddell Chesnutt." The Writer, 11 (August),
　　　　2.
　　　　　Biographical sketch focused on Chesnutt's writing to
　　this date.

5　　ANON. Review of "The Wife of His Youth." Bookman, 7
　　　　(August), 452.

1898

> Chesnutt has a firmer grasp than any other author of the delicate relations between white and black regarding "the mingling of the races." He is the most cultivated and philosophical story writer of the black race.

6 ANON. "The Short Story Season." Kansas City (Missouri) Journal (7 August).
> "The Wife of His Youth" can be read without effort but cannot be forgotten with ease. "Mr. Chesnutt is doing what Mr. Dunbar ought always to do, and that is writing of and for his own people."

7 ANON. "Lytle's Letter." Cleveland Voice (13 August).
> Discusses Chesnutt's recent publishing success and rise to fame. Few men have Chesnutt's opportunity to portray black and white. Thus far, "all of the products of his pen, are quaint in setting, attractive in live situations and sweet and wholesome in plot and expression."

8 ANON. Review of "The Wife of His Youth." Kansas City (Missouri) Star (13 August).
> The story is marked by a fresh and original treatment of life among blacks with social pretensions. The satire is light, poised always between seriousness and mockery.

9 ANON. Untitled article. Bookman, 7 (October), 95-96.
> Discusses Chesnutt's trip to New York in September, to talk with Houghton Mifflin about the publishing of The Conjure Woman. "Mr. Chesnutt's work may not always conform to the popular taste, but there is a classic note in its artistic touch and literary expression which gives it an enduring quality."

1899 A   BOOKS - NONE

1899 B   SHORTER WRITINGS

1 ANON. "Notes About Authors and Their Works." Cleveland Plain Dealer (1 January).
> Considers "The Wife of His Youth" and "Hot-Foot Hanni-bal." The first is one of the most striking stories of the year. The second is a "good story, presenting the Southern negro to the life with his superstitions and mingled cunning, and recalling incidentally the unnatural conditions of Southern social life."

2   ANON. "Literary Gossip." Cleveland <u>Leader</u> (8 January).
         Review of "Hot-Foot Hannibal." The story is better
     than other recent stories in the <u>Atlantic</u> because it deals
     with the superstition that is so prevalent among blacks,
     and because of the humor this subject naturally entails.

3   ANON. Untitled article. Cleveland <u>Index</u> (1 February).
         Chesnutt gave a reading in Cleveland January 21. His
     selection was "'The March of Progress,' a story that would
     have appeared in the January <u>Atlantic</u> in place of 'Hot-Foot
     Hannibal' but for the connection of the latter with the
     general theme of his forthcoming volume." Chesnutt's
     reading was simple, impassioned, and pervaded with quiet
     humor. It greatly pleased the audience.

4   ANON. "Charles W. Chesnutt." Cleveland <u>Recorder</u>
     (13 February).
         Tells of Chesnutt's rise to fame, and of his book soon
     to be released by Houghton Mifflin. Calls "The Wife of
     His Youth," recently published in <u>Atlantic</u>, "one of the
     most remarkable productions recently appearing from the
     pen of any American." It is a classic short story.

5   ANON. "The Conjure Woman." Cleveland <u>Index</u> (15 February).
         "The Wife of His Youth" and "Hot-Foot Hannibal" are
     favorably discussed. The upcoming publication of <u>The Con-
     jure Woman</u> is discussed and Chesnutt's literary skills are
     praised.

6   ANON. Untitled article. Buffalo <u>Express</u> (19 March).
         An announcement that the Rowfant Club of Cleveland will
     publish a special edition of <u>The Conjure Woman</u>.

7   ANON. "The Conjure Woman." Boston <u>Evening Transcript</u>
     (22 March).
         Chesnutt has been able to present both white and black
     fairly. Because of his "blended inheritance," Chesnutt
     can speak "without uncertainty, without romantic gloss,
     without sentimentality." This book marks the appearance
     of a new force in the field of American letters.

8   ANON. Review of <u>The Conjure Woman</u>. St. Louis <u>Globe Democrat</u>
     (25 March).
         Chesnutt has perfectly captured black dialect and has
     an intuitive understanding of black character "with its
     strange mixture of American civilization, and the barbaric
     instincts inherited from African ancestors in the not very
     remote past." Humor is the main note of these stories,
     but underneath lies one of tragedy.

1899

9   ANON. Review of The Conjure Woman. Hartford (Connecticut)
      Post (27 March).
          The book deals with the characteristic superstitions of
      the Anglo-African and is told in inimitable plantation
      dialect. Contains humor, naturalness, and an absence of
      impossible situations.

10   ANON. "A New Afro-American Humorist." Philadelphia Record
      (31 March).
          Review of The Conjure Woman. These are "clever dialect
      tales" all dealing with plantation superstitions in a
      humorous way. They add a new, quaint figure to American
      literature--Uncle Julius McAdoo.

11   ANON. "The Conjure Woman." Cambridge (Massachusetts)
      Tribune (1 April).
          This is a series of tales about the superstitions that
      are, by no means, confined only to blacks in the south.
      Chesnutt knows his topic well, and has introduced into the
      narrative a number of pathetic and humorous incidents,
      illustrating the strange conditions that existed under
      southern slavery. The book presents a way of life that
      has passed away forever.

12   ANON. Review of The Conjure Woman. Boston Saturday Evening
      Gazette (1 April).
          "The author is very successful in his dealing with negro
      dialect, which he describes with much humor and with a
      knowledge born of experience. The stories are all good
      and well worth the reading."

13   ANON. Review of The Conjure Woman. Chicago Journal (1 April).
          It is "a fine instance of North Carolina dialect yarn."
      The "darky talk" is, at times, hard to read, but the tale
      is a good one.

14   ANON. "Some New Books." Nashville Banner (1 April).
          The focus of The Conjure Woman, negro superstitions and
      folklore, is not a new one, but Chesnutt brings to his work
      a new approach. Chesnutt truly writes of his race, for in
      black communities that have not had the enlightening in-
      fluence of education and progress there is still a belief
      in this sort of thing. The chief defect in the book, its
      lack of an intuitive portrayal, stems from Chesnutt's
      perspective as a northerner.

15   ANON. "The Conjure Woman." Boston Courier (2 April).
          The dialect used in these stories is without a flaw.
      The description is true to life. Chesnutt has not only

"pointed out waysides we have not observed before, but he has interpreted them as no one else can."

16 ANON. "The Conjure Woman." Charleston (South Carolina) News (2 April).
These stories are worthy of the pen that wrote "Uncle Remus." Chesnutt has successfully caught the black dialect, and the superstitious characteristics of the black mind. They portray a mingled humor, pathos, and mysticism.

17 ANON. "The Conjure Woman." Cleveland Leader (2 April).
This is a book about the universal superstition that exists in the minds of the black people in the south. It shows the ill effect these beliefs have on the section of the country in which they are found.

18 ANON. "The Conjure Woman." New York Tribune (2 April).
The book is a minor, but amusing performance. Julius McAdoo is a pleasing character, but his tales are often so implausible that it is difficult for the author to soften or excuse them.

19 ANON. "The Conjure Woman." Lincoln (Nebraska) Journal (3 April).
One of the best recent contributions to Afro-American lore. These are stories of negro superstition and strategy. Uncle Julius relates the stories "as circumstances seen to make them necessary to influence his employers and especially his mistress."

20 ANON. "The Conjure Woman." Portland (Maine) Transcript (5 April).
Uncle Julius stands with Uncle Remus as a character of charm and originality. In the stories Julius tells "there is a vein of tragedy and a touch of pathos, yet they are brimming over with humor." One would be hard pressed to find more fresh, vivid, or dramatic stories than these.

21 ANON. "The Mule-Man." Boston Daily Advertiser (5 April).
Review of The Conjure Woman. Focuses on the story "The Conjurer's Revenge" in order to show that Julius' stories are usually told in order to accomplish his own ends.

22 ANON. "Fiction." Troy (New York) Times (7 April).
Review of The Conjure Woman. These stories, although humorous, possess power and dramatic force. The ingenuity with which the tales are told shows Chesnutt to be a writer of far above average ability.

23   ANON. "Strange Superstitions." Minneapolis <u>Journal</u> (8 April).
      Review of <u>The Conjure Woman</u>. This is a book of North
    Carolina negro superstitions. There is good reading and
    much humor in the stories. The negro dialect is "pretty
    generally the real thing."

24   ANON. "The Conjure Woman." Atlanta <u>Constitution</u> (9 April).
      This is a story of the south by a northern author.
    "Of course there are some crudities and mannerisms in the
    style of the author which plainly show that the work is
    not of typically Southern authorship." Nevertheless, the
    portrayal of southern life is usually accurate.

25   ANON. "The Conjure Woman." Denver <u>Times</u> (9 April).
      The stories are so much better than the average stories
    of this kind that they demand attention. Nevertheless, in
    them Chesnutt goes into too much detail in introducing his
    characters and explaining how they came to tell their
    stories. Also, the dialect is often faulty.

26   ANON. "The Conjure Woman." Memphis <u>Commercial Appeal</u>
    (9 April).
      "These conjure stories are all remarkably ingenious,
    and their wild improbabilities are told so plausibly that
    Mr. Chesnutt must be credited with having discovered a new
    and fresh field."

27   ANON. "<u>The Conjure Woman</u>, a Book to Be Read." Cleveland
    <u>Plain Dealer</u> (9 April).
      The claims of this book to special attention do not rest
    on the fact that its author is part negro, although this
    fact has enabled Chesnutt to depict more fully the black
    character. The stories in the book are rich in humor, yet
    there is a note of tragedy. This is even more impressive
    when it is seen that the negro narrator of the stories was
    apparently unconscious of this dimension.

28   ANON. "Plantation Tales." Washington, D. C. <u>Times</u> (9 April).
      <u>The Conjure Woman</u> is a book of plantation tales, tinged
    with voodoo and slave superstition. The stories are brought
    together by Julius McAdoo, a character as impressive as
    Uncle Remus, who often tells the stories as a means to get
    what he wants. This book is an evidence that the truest
    and best pictures of a race are always drawn by a member
    of that race.

29   ANON. Review of <u>The Conjure Woman</u>. New Orleans <u>Daily Picayune</u>
    (9 April).

"The stories are well written, showing familiarity with the whimsicalities and comicalities of negro character, and a subtle perception of the poetry and romance often lying hidden in their hearts."

30 ANON. "Some Tales of Conjuring." Los Angeles Times (9 April).
     Whoever cares for negro dialect will find these tales delightful. "They are full of the unconscious humor, the darky belief in the supernatural, the darky mingled child-likeness and shrewdness."

31 ANON. "The Conjure Woman." Cincinnati Times Star (10 April).
     "The mystic element of the darky character is well brought out and in a manner that presents a graphic picture of slave life. Not the least interesting phase of the tales is the clever way in which old 'Uncle Julius' makes each weird superstition work for his selfish ends."

32 ANON. "The Conjure Woman." Hartford (Connecticut) Courant (11 April).
     "These stories are well told and reflect one side of the negro character that is not generally observed by whites. The dialect is a trifle wearing, but we are getting used to that."

33 ANON. "The Conjure Woman." New Bedford (Massachusetts) Mercury (14 April).
     These stories turn, almost entirely, on the mystical nature of the black mind. They are sometimes weird and tragic, but they are always funny. Chesnutt knows his subject, and if one cares for the dialect that often makes these stories difficult to read, they are enjoyable.

34 ANON. "The Conjure Woman." New York Times (15 April), p. 246.
     The tales are "curious and interesting, and the shrewd-ness with which Uncle Julius relates each one at the moment when it will be most effective in his own interest suggests that the black man is no more above making his superstition profitable than his white brother."

35 ANON. "Hoodooed." Baltimore Sun (15 April).
     Review of The Conjure Woman. "The dialect is not easy reading, but it seems well studied, and all of the tales are acquisitions to our folklore." Two of the best stories are "The Conjurer's Revenge" and "Sis' Becky's Pickaninny."

1899

36   ANON. Review of The Conjure Woman. Boston Beacon (15 April).
        The book has the double attraction of being, at the same
     time, a continuous narrative and a book of short stories.
     It presents one of the most interesting characters of the
     season, Uncle Julius, as well as a number of well drawn
     minor characters. The contrast between the lot of the
     southern whites and blacks is made clearly, but without
     rant.

37   ANON. Review of The Conjure Woman. Outlook, 61 (15 April),
     884.
        The stories are among the most amusing that have been
     seen for a long time, and they give rare insight into negro
     life and character. The humor is contagious and the dia-
     lect is as well done as that in the stories of Joel Chandler
     Harris.

38   ANON. Review of The Conjure Woman. Terre Haute (Indiana)
     Gazette (20 April).
        In these stories, reminiscent of those by Joel Chandler
     Harris, the "dense, savage belief in witchcraft, which
     still beclouds the intellect and hinders the development of
     the colored people of the southern states will be found
     forcibly delineated."

39   ANON. "The Darkey's Belief in Witchcraft." Brooklyn Eagle
     (22 April).
        Review of The Conjure Woman. With this book Chesnutt
     assumes a position in the "front rank" of writers of the
     "New South" in literature. The book well illustrates what
     can be made of the materials of the south, for in it Ches-
     nutt considers the weird folklore and superstition of the
     southern black with a gifted understanding.

40   ANON. "The Conjure Woman." Nashville American (23 April).
        The book is well written, but to the southern reader
     there is a false note in the delineation of the negro char-
     acter. "There seems to be lacking that fullness of under-
     standing which only those born and reared in dominance over
     this particular people can wholly possess."

41   ANON. "The Conjure Woman." St. Paul (Minnesota) Globe
     (23 April).
        "The stories are wonderfully interesting, and show a
     masterly delineation of the black character and its childish
     credulity which make these superstitions such a great part
     of the negro's life."

42   ANON. "The Conjure Woman." Worcester (Massachusetts) Spy
      (23 April).
           The story awakens the delight of the humor and pathos of
      the old slavery days. Though the stories portray a same-
      ness of plot, the details in each one are striking and
      original.

43   ANON. "The Conjure Woman." Philadelphia City and State
      (27 April).
           "The stories remind one of Ruth McEnery Stuart, with
      quite as much humor and knowledge of the negro character;
      but the idea of the Conjure Woman is quite new." The moral
      of the book is an old one and shows the suffering occasioned
      by slavery before the war.

44   ANON. "The Conjure Woman." St. Paul Dispatch (29 April).
           There has been much written both for and against the
      use of dialect in story telling, yet in the hands of Ches-
      nutt it is wholly appropriate. Through this means, Ches-
      nutt is able to present the character of the country in
      which the tales take place, and of the people who live
      there. The narrative style is as fine as Joel Chandler
      Harris', and the central character, Uncle Julius, is as
      good as any ever drawn by Harris.

45   ANON. Review of The Conjure Woman. Philadelphia Press
      (29 April).
           Due to the "negro blood" in his veins, Chesnutt does
      full justice to the black characters he describes. Never-
      theless, the white characters are also presented fairly.
      "The real value in the stories consists in the fact that
      each presents an episode illustrating the more intimate
      phases of the slave life on southern plantations. . . .
      At that time the passive acceptance of conditions . . . by
      the slaves concealed a ferment which the student of psy-
      chology . . . is beginning to understand."

46   ANON. "The Conjure Woman." San Francisco Chronicle
      (30 April).
           The stories combine the genuine flavor of the south, the
      rich reminiscence of the times before the war, and delicious
      humor. They are done with taste and skill and reveal the
      often practical motives of southern black men.

47   ANON. "The Conjure Woman--Truth is Stranger than Fiction."
      Raleigh (North Carolina) News and Observer (30 April).
           This is the best book of short stories of the year. It
      is of particular interest to those in North Carolina,

because it shows a knowledge of the character of southern blacks. The tales are well told by Uncle Julius, and, in terms of dialect stories, they should be ranked with those of Harris and Page. They speak to superstitions that are not peculiar only to blacks.

48   ANON. Review of The Conjure Woman. Springfield (Massachu-setts) Republican (30 April).
      These are delightful bits of humor couched in negro dialect as seductive as that of Harris or Page. "The Goophered Grapevine" is the best story. The dialect in all the stories is rich without being of repellant difficulty.

49   ANON. "The Conjure Woman." Southern Workman, 28 (May), 194-95.
      Perhaps Chesnutt goes a bit too far by attributing also to the conjure woman powers that belong to the witches and wizards of Europe--powers that were never a part of south-ern American folklore. Nevertheless, for literary purposes, Chesnutt's device works well.

50   ANON. "The Conjure Woman." Philadelphia Public Ledger (4 May).
      The tales "depict the shrewdness of the negro in using his superstitions to his own advantage in any traffic with his more enlightened white brother." They portray guile and credulity as the negro works for his own profit with-out any loss of faith in his superstitions.

51   ANON. "Negro Magic." Cincinnati Commercial Tribune (7 May).
      Review of The Conjure Woman. This is a story of the superstitions of North Carolina blacks. The best stories are "Po' Sandy" and "The Conjurer's Revenge." Neverthe-less, the book lacks "the quality that turns bare fact into literature." Although he can put together an interesting book, Chesnutt is not a master like Joel Chandler Harris.

52   ANON. "The Conjure Woman." Chicago Advance (11 May).
      It is a "readable budget of negro superstitions related in the language of some of their sages." The book is not only an entertaining glimpse into black superstitions, it also serves the purpose of "race study."

53   ANON. "A Bright Literary Gem." Washington, D. C. Daily Record (12 May).
      The Conjure Woman tells of the old superstitions of the negro, and on that account alone should be read. Its

strongest appeal, though, is in its beautiful composition
and easy narrative which "weaves the thread of humor into
the thread of pathos."

54 ANON. Untitled article. Chicago Times Herald (12 May).
      A biographical sketch focusing on Chesnutt's literary
work and concluding with an appreciation of The Conjure
Woman.

55 ANON. Untitled article. Troy (New York) Times (12 May).
      A comparison of Chesnutt and Paul Laurence Dunbar.
Chesnutt is now a rival of Dunbar for the honor of being
the greatest black writer of fiction. Indeed, Chesnutt
shows a better appreciation of black traits than does
Dunbar, even though Dunbar is a more graceful writer.

56 ANON. "Charles W. Chesnutt." Washington, D. C. Colored
American (13 May).
      Tells of the very favorable comments The Conjure Woman
is receiving, and of Chesnutt's literary skill. Comments
"with much satisfaction that the gentleman so well com-
mended is an American of African extraction."

57 ANON. "Literary Gossip." Cleveland Leader (14 May).
      An article commenting on the very favorable reception
of Chesnutt's The Conjure Woman across the country. Says
newspapers and prominent journals have praised the book,
and that praise has been even higher in journals and papers
not published in Cleveland, Chesnutt's home town.

58 ANON. Review of The Conjure Woman. Boston Congregationalist
(18 May).
      "The superstitious belief in witchcraft and magic which
used to pervade the colored people in the South so largely
comes to light in these stories, which are amusing blend-
ings of the grave and comical. Not the least of the at-
tractions of the book is the droll way in which the under-
lying purpose of Uncle Julius in telling his stories is
revealed from time to time."

59 ANON. "Charles W. Chesnutt." Brooklyn Times (20 May).
      A biographical sketch of Chesnutt in order to acquaint
people with the life and work of a writer who has recently
attracted a good deal of attention by reason of his subtle
understanding and appreciation of negro character and
traits.

1899

60 ANON. "Charles W. Chesnutt." Book Buyer, 18 (June), 360-61.
      A portrait of Chesnutt and "a sketch of his life which
    is interesting as showing the gradual development of
    literary power in a man whose busy life has been spent,
    until now, in other pursuits."

61 ANON. "Chronicle and Comment." Bookman, 9 (June), 295-96.
      Biographical sketch, and critical comment about The Con-
    jure Woman. Standing between two races, Chesnutt can well
    deal with life on the old plantation which often consisted
    of an intense current "smothered beneath a careless ex-
    terior of seemingly passive acceptance of the existing
    order of things."

62 ANON. Review of The Conjure Woman. Bookman, 9 (June), 372-73.
      The keynote of all the stories is the blind superstition
    and duplicity fostered by a life of servility to a slave
    system. Thus these stories represent an impartial picture
    of the life of a slave in the south. If Uncle Julius' be-
    havior is a bit morally questionable, it is probably the
    result of his close association with the white man. This
    is a remarkable tale, told from the perspective of a
    plantation black.

63 ANON. "Romance's Dark Side." Southern Farm Magazine (June),
    12.
      A review of The Conjure Woman. In this age of stress,
    romantic literature and history often appeal to readers be-
    cause it does not deal with the hard, unpleasant facts of
    life. Such has been a reason for some of the success of
    black dialect stories. Chesnutt uses the same southern
    background on which to color his pictures, but, unlike
    other similar writers, Chesnutt has focused on black field
    workers, not house servants, and he has allowed Uncle
    Julius a shrewd purpose in spinning his yarns. Thus "he
    has written a book attractive in itself, but possessing
    more than usual interest for readers who depend upon fic-
    tion to aid them in reaching full, historic truth and who
    wish to know both sides."

64 ANON. Review of The Conjure Woman. Nation, 68 (1 June), 421.
      The stories in this book are "delightfully frank in
    their supernaturalism." The fact that Uncle Julius relates
    these stories for his own benefit "cannot rob one of the
    belief that this was the real religion of the old planta-
    tion; the goopher 'mixtry,' not the overseer's lash, the
    dreaded power."

65   ANON. "The Conjure Woman." Chicago <u>Record</u> (10 June).
      "The tales are primarily stories of conjury, but cannot
      be said to disclose very much inventive faculty or the
      imaginative quality which has enabled some dialect writers
      of the south to invest their fiction's yarns with humor and
      quaint interest."

66   ANON. "The Conjure Woman." Pittsburg <u>Bulletin</u> (10 June).
      "The various 'hants' furnish a tolerable good foundation
      for the little tales, but they lack the picturesqueness of
      the Anglo-Saxon ghost; one merely gets the negro idea, not
      any really ghostly, spooky, or psychical amusement such as
      the mind of the white man can play with."

67   ANON. Untitled article. Boston <u>Literary World</u> (10 June).
      An article telling of the success of <u>The Conjure Woman</u>
      and of the fact that a new book by Chesnutt will soon
      follow it.

68   ANON. Review of <u>The Conjure Woman</u>. New York <u>Public Opinion</u>
      (15 June).
      With this book Chesnutt shows himself the rival of Ruth
      McEnery Stuart and Joel Chandler Harris. The central
      character, Uncle Julius, is as good as was ever invented
      and marvelously believable.

69   ANON. "Houghton, Mifflin and Co." New York <u>Mail and Express</u>
      (17 June).
      Review of <u>The Conjure Woman</u>. Chesnutt "has succeeded
      in overcoming the difficulty upon which so many efforts
      have been shipwrecked; he presents the negro mind as it
      works and suppresses entirely the Caucasion point of view,
      which would make a study of it incorrect."

70   ANON. Review of <u>The Conjure Woman</u>. St. Joseph (Missouri)
      <u>Herald</u> (18 June).
      The stories are full of charm and quaint humor. The
      character of Uncle Julius is well done and the scenes and
      customs that are portrayed are excellent. The stories com-
      pare favorably with those of Thomas Nelson Page.

71   ANON. "The Conjure Woman." New York <u>Commercial Advertiser</u>
      (20 June).
      In looking at this book one must put aside all questions
      of slavery and look at the stories only as a contribution
      to American folklore dealing with the superstitions of the
      black American. Nevertheless, the book must be recognized
      as a limited contribution. It is not a work of art, like

the stories of Joel Chandler Harris. Its best stories are:
"The Goophered Grapevine," "Po' Sandy," "Mars Jeems's
Nightmare," and "The Conjurer's Revenge."

72 ANON. Review of The Conjure Woman. Literary World, 30
(24 June), 204.
These stories are remarkably interesting. They focus on
superstition and magic and exemplify the way in which con-
stant association with this sort of thing works upon minds
ordinarily beyond it.

73 ANON. "Stories of Negro Superstitions." San Francisco
Argonaut (26 June).
The Conjure Woman must have been as hard to write, given
the dialect that is used, as it is to read. Despite this
problem, the stories are humorous and interesting.

74 ANON. Review of The Conjure Woman. Critic, 35 (July), 650.
The outlook of the author is alien to the race and section treated in the book. One must conclude that Chesnutt
is out of sympathy with the developments of the plantation.
This is why the character Julius is not entirely rounded
out and why, perhaps, his selfish character is emphasized.
There is little humor here. Uncle Julius is as "grim and
uncompromising in his selfish designs as the whitest rascal
ever born."

75 ANON. Review of The Conjure Woman. Outlook, 62 (1 July), 540.
The seven stories are full of marvelous things. Chesnutt has a gift for story telling, a shrewd humor, an eye
for comic effects, and an unfaltering artistic sense.
Chesnutt knows his material well.

76 ANON. Review of The Conjure Woman. Augusta (Georgia)
Chronicle (4 July).
None have made the black man more humorous than Chesnutt. Uncle Julius will become as popular as Uncle Remus
because of his "rich, lazy dialect, his characteristic
dark garrulousness, and his cunning consciousness of the
effect of his yarns."

77 ANON. "The Conjure Woman." Richmond (Virginia) Times
(7 July).
This is a book about the south written from the point
of view of an Ohioan. Chesnutt writes regarding matters
about which he knows nothing, and concerning which he has
unfortunate and unjust views. The south should be left to
a less biased observer.

78   ANON. "Book Chat." St. Louis (Missouri) Globe Democrat
       (9 July).
         An examination of the use of the supernatural by the
       southern black man, and a comment that this phenomenon is
       examined in Chesnutt's book The Conjure Woman. "Whether
       the African ghost is a discovery or an evolution is of no
       particular consequence. . . . Its principal uses are to
       keep the southern darky in a state of mind bordering on
       lunacy."

79   ANON. "A Forcible Writer." Cleveland Gazette (9 July).
         Remarks favorably on Chesnutt's article titled "What Is
       a White Man?" in the May Independent. Tells of Chesnutt's
       life in Cleveland, and of his excellent future prospects.

80   ANON. Untitled article. New York Times (23 July).
         "I am afraid we will have to change our opinion of the
       negro: he has learned to write." Paul Laurence Dunbar
       and Chesnutt have arisen to break down the white man's
       stereotypes. "These two young authors have done more to
       justify the education of the negro than all the preaching
       and exhorting since the civil war."

81   ANON. "Something About the Author of the Conjure Woman."
       New York Age (27 July).
         A biographical sketch which focuses on Chesnutt's close
       association with his race.

82   ANON. "The Conjure Woman." Augusta (Georgia) Herald
       (31 July).
         No stories of this kind have met with more acceptance
       than those of Joel Chandler Harris. "Both the matter and
       the manner of the telling are irresistible, and having been
       once met, it is impossible to bid Julius farewell until he
       has nothing more to say."

83   ANON. Review of The Conjure Woman. Current Literature, 26
       (August), 124.
         This is a series of stories having their motive in black
       superstition, and tied together by an old man who tells
       tales for his own benefit.

84   ANON. "The Conjure Woman." Cambridge (Massachusetts)
       Chronicle (15 August).
         A "capital collection" of stories. Chesnutt's "happy
       faculty" for catching the spoken dialect and the interest-
       ing focus make this an entertaining volume.

1899

85 ANON. "Charles W. Chesnutt." Book Buyer, 19 (September),
    84-85.
        An appreciative comment about The Conjure Woman and a
    notice that Chesnutt is currently contemplating two books,
    The Wife of His Youth, and Frederick Douglass. "No writer
    in the country is more competent" to write about Douglass.

86 ANON. "The Conjure Woman." Jacksonville (Florida) Times
    Mirror Citizen (10 September).
        These stories deal with old time, ignorant superstition,
    are amusing in the extreme, are told well in dialect, and
    their very ridiculousness incites interest. "The Con-
    jurer's Revenge" is the foremost.

87 ANON. "The Negro in the South." Boston Transcript
    (20 September).
        Tells of a speech given by Chesnutt regarding the posi-
    tion of blacks in the south. Primarily a historical talk,
    it traced the situation of the southern black man since his
    first arrival in the United States. The question of para-
    mount importance today, said Chesnutt, is whether or not
    the gains of the civil war and since shall be nullified by
    racial prejudice, a situation which the southern white man
    would be only too happy to bring about.

88 ANON. Review of The Conjure Woman. Independent, 51
    (21 September), 2569-70.
        "A very enjoyable little book." The oddities and
    drollery of black life are well depicted and there is much
    freshness of incident and dialogue.

89 ANON. "Bethel Literary." Washington, D. C. Daily Record
    (22 November).
        Favorable account of a reading given by Chesnutt. Ches-
    nutt was followed on the platform by P. B. S. Pinchback,
    Lewis Douglass, and Archibald Grimke, who commented quite
    favorably on the good accomplished by Chesnutt's writings.

90 ANON. Review of The Conjure Woman. Washington, D. C. Colored
    American (25 November).
        "They ain't na'er a book in the dialect language, that
    can 'proach it in originality, naturalness, and trueness to
    the life of the negro of the day before yesterday. It has
    a flavor which only a negro writer could give to a collec-
    tion of the folklore of the race. . . . The white folks
    who write dialect are not in it with the men of our race."

91   ANON. Review of <u>The Wife of His Youth</u>. Burlington (Iowa)
     <u>Hawk Eye</u> (1 December).
          "These short stories demonstrate the fact that much
     sorrow and needless suffering has been caused by the with-
     drawal of the 'color line,' and the mingling of the races."

92   ANON. Review of <u>The Wife of His Youth</u>. Nashville <u>Banner</u>
     (2 December).
          Chesnutt's book <u>The Conjure Woman</u> was well received in
     the south, for the stories were true to life pictures of
     the southern black. This volume is a disappointment.
     Chesnutt has abandoned the south and appears to favor mis-
     cegenation, or at least relaxing the white attitude. This
     will not appeal to whites anywhere.

93   ANON. Review of <u>The Wife of His Youth</u>. Bridgeport
     (Connecticut) <u>Standard</u> (4 December).
          Chesnutt's writing vies with that of Thomas Nelson Page,
     Paul Laurence Dunbar, Joel Chandler Harris, and Booker T.
     Washington. His work has far more literary merit than that
     usually associated with stories in his field.

94   ANON. Review of <u>The Wife of His Youth</u>. Boston <u>Journal</u>
     (6 December).
          Chesnutt's first book of "delicious plantation legends"
     surpassed even the stories of Joel Chandler Harris and
     Thomas Nelson Page. This book is different from the first
     one, but the stories in it have the same "suggestion of
     reality, the same flavor, the same mingling of gaiety and
     gloom, the same interest."

95   ANON. Review of <u>Frederick Douglass</u>. Boston <u>Watchman</u>
     (7 December).
          "It is a just tribute and a fair portrait of a character
     remarkable from any point of view." This volume fills a
     unique place and possesses a positive value.

96   ANON. Review of <u>Frederick Douglass</u>. Buffalo <u>Enquirer</u>
     (9 December).
          Despite the brevity of this book, it does full justice
     to the noble character of Douglass. The strongest features
     of his remarkable personality, and the influence he exerted
     over the course of historical events are portrayed. This
     is a thorough study and a necessary one.

97   ANON. Review of <u>Frederick Douglass</u>. Nashville <u>Banner</u>
     (9 December).
          Chesnutt is a happy choice to write this biography be-
     cause he is not only sympathetic to his subject, but both

1899

he and Douglass lean toward the doctrine of miscegenation.
In order to create sympathy for Douglass, Chesnutt has gone
out of his way to paint the horrors of slavery, and he
makes statements which are hardly credible. This biography
would be better if it was relieved of some of Chesnutt's
prejudices.

98 ANON. Review of The Wife of His Youth. New York Mail and
Express (9 December).
There is a variation here on the usual method employed
by those who write about American blacks. Instead of try-
ing to move the reader's compassion for the black man, or
to make the black man likeable by appearing comical and
childlike, it simply aims to interest the reader in the
black man as an individual human being, without regard to
the color of his skin.

99 ANON. Review of Frederick Douglass. Buffalo Express
(10 December).
An admirable short biography of Douglass. "It is plain,
lucid, devotes its space to the narration of fact and not
sermonizing, and its selection of facts is such as to show
the career of its subject in proper proportion."

100 ANON. Review of The Wife of His Youth. Cleveland Plain
Dealer (10 December).
This book strikes a deeper and stronger note than did
The Conjure Woman. It is not as light and amusing as was
the former volume, and deals more insistently with the
perplexing problems of the color line.

101 ANON. Review of The Wife of His Youth. Los Angeles Herald
(10 December).
"This volume is in all ways good, with some passages
that show actual genius." The strongest stories in the
book are "The Wife of His Youth," "A Matter of Principle,"
and "The Blue Vein Society." ["The Blue Vein Society"
does not appear in this book.]

102 ANON. Review of The Wife of His Youth. San Francisco
Bulletin (10 December).
Chesnutt "may be forgiven for idealizing his jet heroes
and heroines since that is a caucasian failing." But he
has not exaggerated the black man's love of justice and
fidelity. The book is a "pathetic and original" plea for
brotherhood.

103   ANON. Review of <u>The Wife of His Youth</u>. Portland (Maine)
        <u>Advertiser</u> (13 December).
            Chesnutt is one of the few writers who can produce good
        stories about American blacks. In this book, Chesnutt
        "shows himself possessed of many of the most important
        qualities essential to the successful writer of fiction;
        and one of these is the combination of an excellent style
        with a distinct gift to interest readers."

104   ANON. "Some Christmas Books." St. Louis (Missouri) <u>Mirror</u>
        (14 December).
            Review of <u>The Wife of His Youth</u>. "It's as sweet as the
        'Swanee Ribber,' or 'Old Folks at Home,' and, like them,
        justifies the negro's existence upon earth and all his suf-
        ferings in the past and all his aspirations in the future."

105   ANON. Review of <u>The Wife of His Youth</u>. Boston <u>Christian</u>
        <u>Register</u> (14 December).
            The quality of Chesnutt's work makes him one of the most
        interesting of American fiction writers. He portrays his
        own race faithfully and with care. His work stands with
        that of Booker T. Washington and Paul Laurence Dunbar.

106   ANON. "Chesnutt's Tales." Boston <u>Transcript</u> (16 December).
            Review of <u>The Wife of His Youth</u>. The simplicity with
        which Chesnutt tells his tales befits the "primitive motive
        which makes their pathetic interest." The narrator is never
        bitter, and thus each situation is presented to the reader
        more vividly than it would be otherwise. "The Bouquet" is
        the best story in the book.

107   ANON. Review of <u>Frederick Douglass</u>. Rochester <u>Democrat</u>
        <u>Chronicle</u> (16 December).
            This is a biography which no library should lack. It is
        given color and life by Chesnutt's "avowed heart-interest"
        in his subject and by his "profound . . . sympathy with
        every step of Douglass's upward career." This is "an epic
        which finds few to equal it in either romance or reality."

108   ANON. Review of <u>The Wife of His Youth</u>. Philadelphia <u>Times</u>
        (16 December).
            There is much that is explanatory about the black man
        here. Despite the fact that some of these stories are a
        bit didactic, there is no moral drawn in any of them except
        that which the reader can get from the facts. It will sur-
        prise most people to see how far race mixing has occurred,
        and how such definite rules have evolved with regard to it.

1899

109   ANON. Review of <u>The Wife of His Youth</u>. St. Louis <u>Globe</u>
          (16 December).
              "The various types of the race are well portrayed, and
          the high ideals the author would inculcate are in striking
          contrast to the 'coon' propensities with which fiction and
          the stage have made us so familiar."

110   ANON. Review of <u>The Wife of His Youth</u>. Mobile (Alabama)
          <u>Register</u> (17 December).
              Unlike Chesnutt's first collection of stories, this one
          deals with northern blacks. It is interesting to see how
          the "blue vein" blacks discriminate more against pure blacks
          than the whites do. This book, and the one that preceded
          it, will not achieve great popularity in the south.

111   ANON. Review of <u>The Wife of His Youth</u>. Springfield (Massa-
          chusetts) <u>Republican</u> (17 December).
              Those who usually approach dialect stories "with fear
          and trembling" need have no alarm from this book, for it
          deals with characters who are almost white and speak in
          elegant English. There is real tragedy to the situation of
          these people Chesnutt describes, for they are compelled to
          mingle with people of an inferior race to which they are
          only remotely akin.

112   ANON. Review of <u>Frederick Douglass</u>. Washington, D. C. <u>Times</u>
          (19 December).
              Chesnutt is as successful in this biography as he has
          previously been with his stories. It is brief, concise,
          comprehensive, and sympathetic. Throughout the book Ches-
          nutt has made reflections on the position of the negro in
          the United States, and these comments are a welcome
          addition.

113   ANON. "Mr. Chesnutt Finds a New Phase in the Southern Race
          Question." Boston <u>Evening Transcript</u> (20 December).
              A review of <u>The Wife of His Youth</u>. Deals particularly
          with the title story, which is said to be the strongest.
          The central question of the story is should a person who
          is a small part black be bound to regard himself as a
          black.

114   ANON. "The Negro's Place in American Fiction: Interesting
          Stories by Charles W. Chesnutt." Louisville <u>Times</u>
          (20 December).
              With the changing times the old "plantation darky" is
          passing from American literature. He is being replaced by
          a new black man, a "post-bellum darky," and this character

is now being fictionalized by black writers like Chesnutt and Paul Laurence Dunbar. The Wife of His Youth is discussed as an example of this new approach.

115   ANON. Review of The Wife of His Youth. Cambridge (Massachusetts) Tribune (23 December).
       At last with the advent of writers like Chesnutt one can know the black man as he is known to those of his own race. Chesnutt's stories all reveal his feelings regarding the injustices inflicted on his race, but his arraignment of the white race is, in these works, by implication rather than by direct attack.

116   ANON. Review of Frederick Douglass. Providence (Rhode Island) Journal (24 December).
       The book furnishes a "brief, readable and authentic account" of a man who has impressed himself deeply on the character and history of his country.

117   ANON. Review of Frederick Douglass. Springfield (Massachusetts) Republican (24 December).
       Chesnutt is an appropriate writer to pay homage to Douglass for Chesnutt has "an intelligent interest in the negro race." In the book, Chesnutt has shown Douglass "very fairly, and his book gives an impression of the powerful physical and intellectual make-up of this gifted orator."

118   ANON. Review of The Wife of His Youth. Cleveland Leader (24 December).
       Makes much of the fact that Chesnutt, a Cleveland author, is publishing in major magazines and being reviewed favorably across the nation. The story "A Matter of Principle" is quoted at length.

119   ANON. "Stories of the Negro in The Wife of His Youth." Chicago Times (24 December).
       The book is characterized by genuine sympathy for the black man and an ability to make a point. The tales contained in the book are quite remarkable, displaying much drama and pathos. The stories most worthy of mention are "The Wife of His Youth," "The Sheriff's Children," and "The Web of Circumstance."

120   ANON. Review of Frederick Douglass. Boston Journal (25 December).
       This is a handsome tribute to Douglass, both appreciative and well written. Chesnutt has made the most of his

1899

opportunities here, and, since he also has negro blood, it is fitting that he has done so.

121 ANON. Review of Frederick Douglass. Chicago Chronicle (25 December).
    The book confines itself closely to narrative fact, yet "continues to wear the heroic atmosphere. . . . At all events the outline of his life is to be found here and with something too much of a halo about it; one may readily make allowance, as must be done in reading so much other anti-slavery literature."

122 ANON. Review of Frederick Douglass. Pittsburg Times (30 December).
    "The style and finish of the book, and the evidences which it bears of the accomplished literary workman, may be instanced as a part of the fruit of Douglass's struggle for freedom and opportunity for his race."

123 ANON. Review of The Wife of His Youth. St. Paul (Minnesota) Globe (31 December).
    "Mr. Chesnutt looks at his darkies as one would look at a chinaman or a savage. So there seems to be something lacking in his treatment. He does not seem to get a heart into his characters."

124 BOUVRE, PAULENE CARRINGTON. "An Aboriginal Author." Boston Transcript (23 August).
    A biographical sketch and interview with Chesnutt. Chesnutt's heritage is emphasized. "The Wife of His Youth" is discussed, and Chesnutt's views on "the race problem" are put forth. He suggests that the solution to this problem will only come through "education and enlightenment."

125 EARLE, MARY TRACY. Review of The Conjure Woman. Book Buyer, 18 (June), 401.
    This book can only be compared to "Uncle Remus," but it takes up such a different set of traditions that it is better to make no comparisons at all. The story focuses on Uncle Julius, who always has a quite natural reason for telling his stories; he wants to have things his own way.

126 LANDON. "Negro Authors and Professionals." New York Evening Post (12 August).
    Chesnutt is prominently mentioned as a notable black man, in a consideration of the position of blacks in contemporary American society. While conditions still often hinder the black man, it is suggested that he is quickly

climbing the social and economic ladder. Chesnutt is but one example.

127   SHIPMAN, CAROLYN. "The Author of 'The Conjure Woman,' Charles W. Chesnutt." Critic, 35 (July), 632.
       A biographical sketch prompted by the very favorable reception that The Conjure Woman is receiving. Focuses on Chesnutt's literary development and lauds him for his non-partisan view of the problems of race.

1900 A BOOKS - NONE

1900 B SHORTER WRITINGS

1   ANON. Review of The Wife of His Youth. Topeka (Kansas) Journal (1 January).
     This is a fine book of strong short stories. "These stories will only go on to prove, as did 'The Conjure Woman,' Mr. Chesnutt's ability, power, and literary skill as a story writer."

2   ANON. Review of Frederick Douglass. Philadelphia City and State (4 January).
     "No one can read it without being impressed by the importance of Douglass' cause, and if Mr. Chesnutt's enthusiasm makes him seem to sympathize too deeply with the spirit of revolt, it awakens an echo in the heart of everyone who loves liberty for its own sake."

3   ANON. Review of The Wife of His Youth. New York Christian Advocate (4 January).
     "While there is no exploiting of his own race, as is the manner with some other writers, he shows a deep sympathy with and complete understanding of their difficult problems."

4   ANON. "In the Borderland." Washington, D. C. Times (7 January).
     Review of The Wife of His Youth, and comment on stories about the south in general. Many have tried their hand at this type of story, but few have succeeded. Chesnutt is one of the successful, for he writes as no "outsider" could of the black people. The book has two main faults. It presents as typical some incidents which are not, and there is a subtly sarcastic tone to some of the sketches.

1900

5   ANON.   "A New Author of Good Stories of Southern Life."
    San Francisco Chronicle (7 January).
        Review of The Wife of His Youth. Chesnutt's work out-
    ranks that of all writers of the south except Joel Chandler
    Harris. This second book is good, and each story brings
    out a "new trait of the negro race."

6   ANON.   Review of Frederick Douglass. Minneapolis Times
    (7 January).
        Perhaps the reason that this book has such a vivid in-
    terest is that it was written by a negro about a negro
    hero. This book should be written by a black, and it
    makes us feel that the negro has "arrived." "What Mr.
    Washington is doing for the material and social side of
    the negro's progress, Mr. Chesnutt is doing for the
    spiritual side."

7   ANON.   Review of Frederick Douglass. Portland (Maine)
    Transcript (10 January).
        Questions Chesnutt's account of Douglass' parentage.
    Suggests that Douglass' powerful character came to him
    from his grandmother, who was a full-blooded Potomac
    Indian.

8   ANON.   Review of Frederick Douglass. Boston Advertiser
    (12 January).
        "Within this brief compass Mr. Chesnutt has contrived
    to present the chief events of the life of the most dis-
    tinguished of American negroes; and at the same time, to
    give the fascinating story the appearance of completeness
    in detail. It is eulogistic as it ought to be, as it must
    be, if truthful; but is at the same time discriminative."

9   ANON.   Review of The Wife of His Youth. Troy (New York)
    Times (12 January).
        This book is not quite as good as The Conjure Woman.
    It deals with the north, and not the south, and thus is
    not as picturesque. "Indeed, if the illustrations were
    omitted from the book, it is doubtful if the average
    reader would see in it anything more than a delineation
    of very prosaic white society."

10 ANON.   "Frederick Douglass." New York Times Book Review
    (13 January), p. 20.
        A favorable review of the book. Tells of Douglass'
    life and achievements and concludes: "He was so busy that
    the bare record of his work occupies nearly all the book,
    and Mr. Chesnutt has deviated little from it, adorning it

with the briefest touches of anecdote or epithet, and
probably has come nearer to the real man than any one who
has described him."

11 ANON. Review of The Wife of His Youth. Boston Beacon
    (13 January).
        The book presents "some of the most pitiful things that
    have ever been written." These have to do with people who
    "will not class themselves with blacks and yet are not
    recognized socially as members of the white race." Some
    of the stories illustrate the white man's disposition re-
    garding the mixing of race and some show "the childlike
    traits of the blacks."

12 ANON. Review of The Wife of His Youth. Brooklyn Eagle
    (20 January).
        "One is accustomed to thinking of darkies as all dark,
    . . . but these tales teach that there are many degrees of
    caste among them, the highest and haughtiest being those of
    light skin, and that the greatest ambition of these
    classes . . . is to marry pure whites, and their lowest
    state is to degrade themselves by marrying full-blooded
    negroes."

13 ANON. Untitled article. Tuskeegee (Alabama) Student
    (20 January).
        In an article about the coming of age of black litera-
    ture, Chesnutt is mentioned as the writer of "a number of
    the most brilliant short stories which have appeared in
    any American publication" during the last years. Both The
    Conjure Woman and The Wife of His Youth are mentioned
    favorably.

14 ANON. Review of The Wife of His Youth. Boston Courier
    (21 January).
        Chesnutt is to be congratulated, for his book deals with
    present conditions. He presents "the negro problem" in the
    most forceful way it can be presented, not by arguing it,
    but by simply presenting the black "condition of mind and
    how they regard themselves and whites."

15 ANON. Review of The Wife of His Youth. Nashville American
    (21 January).
        This book stands in marked contrast to Booker T. Wash-
    ington's advice to the black man to be satisfied in ele-
    vating himself rather than to "enter a life which is not
    his." These stories show a good literary style, but ex-
    press an unreal ambition. These stories do not show the

black man at his best, and one resents the unnatural life of the people portrayed and their false ambitions.

16   ANON. "Charles W. Chesnutt." Brooklyn Times (27 January).
      A biographical sketch giving information about the writer whose work has lately attracted so much attention.

17   ANON. Review of Frederick Douglass. Indianapolis News (27 January).
      This sketch is admirably sympathetic and gives the reader a vivid picture of Douglass. The opening chapters of the biography are particularly well done, and are of particular interest.

18   ANON. Review of Frederick Douglass. San Francisco News (27 January).
      Primarily a recounting of Douglass' life. Calls the book "full of interest" and says that it presents the indispensable life of "the champion of an oppressed race." This will "serve as an incentive to aspiring souls."

19   ANON. "Fiction and Fact." Wilmington (North Carolina) Messenger (28 January).
      Attempts to correct the false facts presented in Chesnutt's story "The Bouquet," published in the November, 1899, issue of the Atlantic. Claims that the scene of the story was Fayetteville, North Carolina, but that few of the deplorable situations Chesnutt describes actually happened.

20   ANON. Review of The Wife of His Youth. Critic, 36 (February), 182.
      "The stories bring home the solemn truth that no man lives for himself alone. Even though he rises socially and intellectually, he has responsibilities of family and race which he cannot shake off." The subject matter of this book is distinctively better than that of The Conjure Woman. It is a consideration of the struggle which has already begun in the north and thus it is timely. Hopefully Chesnutt will soon free himself from his colloquialisms.

21   ANON. Review of Frederick Douglass. New York Churchman (3 February).
      This is a "readable narrative." The book is temperate in its judgments of Douglass' contemporaries, and is sympathetic in its appreciation of Douglass' natural genius.

22   ANON. Review of The Wife of His Youth. Brooklyn Times (3 February).

Chesnutt takes an unusual approach. He portrays the
black man as a person, "not as a being of a race apart,
but as a part of the great human family we call mankind.
. . . The stories have humor and pathos, but neither emo-
tion grows out of the fact that the personages are other
than men and women."

23   ANON. Review of The Wife of His Youth. Philadelphia Press
      (3 February).
      Thus far no writers have been able to deal with the
      issue of the race problem adequately. Due to his race,
      Chesnutt succeeds now, where Cable, Howells, and Kingsley
      have not. Chesnutt's book is a strong one. Its faults
      are the faults of a beginner and they are easily hidden by
      the powerful conception of the book, which presents the
      difficult situation of the mulatto.

24   ANON. Review of The Wife of His Youth. Brooklyn Citizen
      (4 February).
      Chesnutt opens an unexplored area with these stories,
      for the book is not only a novel, but a contribution to the
      race question as well. The value of the book lies in the
      fact that it portrays the black man as a human being.

25   ANON. Review of The Wife of His Youth. Cleveland World
      (4 February).
      Cleveland is proud of Chesnutt. His new book will only
      add to his reputation. "Her Virginia Mammy" is the best
      story in the collection, but others are very good.

26   ANON. Review of The Wife of His Youth. Springfield (Ohio)
      Mail and Express (4 February).
      Chesnutt has opened "a wholly new and hitherto unex-
      plored field in literature." The stories in this book are
      unique because they present the black man as a human being,
      without the exaggerated pathos of the purpose novel or the
      exaggerated humor of the "negro story."

27   ANON. "Our Story-Telling Chesnutt." Cleveland Plain Dealer
      (11 February).
      A cartoon of Chesnutt, who stands on a winged book with
      the following caption: "Out of the local burr you rise,/
      Your stories gladden countless eyes;/ And proudly here we
      watch you soar,/ Bright genius from old Erie's shore."

28   ANON. Review of The Wife of His Youth. Literary World, 31
      (17 February), 55.

1900

These stories of "colored life" show a rich variety.
All the characters are portrayed by the hand of an intimate
acquaintance. "The Wife of His Youth" and "The Bouquet"
are particularly noteworthy.

29　ANON. Review of The Wife of His Youth. San Francisco Western
Outlook (20 February).
"Each story is a gem from beginning to end and there is
not an uninteresting page." Chesnutt shows familiarity
with the race question, and presents peculiarities of
character without exaggeration or embellishment.

30　ANON. Review of The Wife of His Youth. Chicago Advance
(22 February).
This book tells the "sad story" of the conditions of
black Americans. Chesnutt's books are among the most interpretive volumes recently published regarding American
blacks, but as stories, the tales in this volume have little
worth. They are valuable as interpretations of the character and condition of American blacks.

31　ANON. Review of The Wife of His Youth. Chicago Interior
(22 February).
"The stories are all readable, and some are eminently
good." Chesnutt abstains from partisan pleas in them, even
though his points are strong. "A Matter of Principle" is
the best story in the book. Indeed, all the stories are
good with the exception of "Her Virginia Mammy," which is
mawkish.

32　ANON. Review of The Wife of His Youth. Philadelphia Church
Standard (24 February).
These stories are very good, but unless Chesnutt is a
black man, writing for blacks, nine black stories in one
volume is too much. If Chesnutt is black, then what he has
done is all right, but he should let himself be known as a
black man. Despite the fact that these stories were quite
good, the reviewer could only read through half of them.

33　ANON. Review of The Wife of His Youth. Boston Congregationalist (1 March).
"They are fresh and entertaining stories, evidently
based upon close observation of the differences between
the mulattos and the darker Negroes, and portraying inter-
estingly their special ambitions and the peculiar conditions
of their life."

34   ANON. Review of <u>The Wife of His Youth</u>. San Francisco
      <u>Argonaut</u> (12 March).
           "Mr. Chesnutt writes with no little power, and though
      there is sentiment and pathos in all his sketches, they
      ring true in nearly every instance."

35   ANON. Review of <u>Frederick Douglass</u>. Boston <u>Christian World</u>
      (15 March).
           "The book is a stirring reminder of stirring times, and
      a fine portrait of one of the noblest men God ever made."

36   ANON. "Progress of a Race." New York <u>Mail and Express</u>
      (17 March).
           An account of a meeting between Chesnutt and Booker T.
      Washington, at which the progress of the race was discussed.
      Chesnutt's views on the amalgamation of the races are men-
      tioned, and <u>The Wife of His Youth</u> is considered in light of
      a contemporary court case in which the same issue is at
      stake.

37   ANON. "Scholarship and Prize for Atlanta." Boston <u>Record</u>
      (22 March).
           Tells of a dinner given for Chesnutt and R. L. Smith,
      in order to raise money for an Atlanta University scholar-
      ship fund.

38   ANON. Review of <u>Frederick Douglass</u>. Baltimore <u>News</u> (9 April).
           Focuses on Chesnutt's view of Douglass' birth and early
      life. Suggests that Douglass did not owe his intellectual
      abilities to the black side of his family.

39   ANON. Review of <u>The Wife of His Youth</u>. Boston <u>Christian
      World</u> (12 April).
           Chesnutt's book entitles him to a wreath like that be-
      longing to Joel Chandler Harris. All the stories in it
      are "master delineations of a race piquant enough to test
      the powers of the greatest artist."

40   ANON. "A New Writer." Jacksonville (Florida) <u>Times Union
      Citizen</u> (29 April).
           A general appreciation of Chesnutt's life and writing.
      Tells of the favorable reception accorded <u>The Wife of His
      Youth</u>, of Chesnutt's voluntary association with his race,
      of his objective treatment of racial issues in his stories,
      and of Howells' favorable reviews of Chesnutt's work.

41   ANON. "W. D. Howells on Charles W. Chesnutt." Cleveland
      <u>Plain Dealer</u> (29 April).

1900

>Tells of Howells' praise for Chesnutt's writings and quotes extensively from Howells' <u>Atlantic</u> review of Chesnutt.

42 ANON. "Objectionable Stories." Cincinnati <u>Commercial Tribune</u> (13 May).
>Review of <u>The Wife of His Youth</u>. Chesnutt is not at all able to write fiction. He should declare himself in essays, not draw out his opinions in stories. All the stories in the volume are poor. "They deal with matters which are repulsive or strangely morbidly sad."

43 ANON. "A Gifted Writer of Stories." Boston <u>Herald</u> (14 May).
>A biographical and critical sketch, together with a notice that Chesnutt is presently in Boston.

44 ANON. "The Trail of the Ethiopian." <u>Literary Review</u>, 4 (15 May), 1.
>Chesnutt is mentioned as one of "the best of his kind," in an article that states "the real negro is not a human being at all. . . . He merits a place in literature only because of his acute and terrible depravity." In light of the propensities of the race, Chesnutt's genius makes little difference. "There has always been an eminent negro or two in every generation; . . . but they are not signs of a race's progress. They are simply freaks of fate."

45 ANON. "Charles W. Chesnutt's Stories." <u>Current Literature</u>, 28 (June), 277-78.
>Discusses <u>The Conjure Woman</u>, <u>The Wife of His Youth</u>, and <u>Frederick Douglass</u>. The last is said to be "a simple, solid, straight piece of work not remarkable above many other biographical studies . . . yet important as the work of a man not entirely white." The stories in the other books are said to be generally quite good. "These stories are important whether we consider them merely realistic fiction, apart from their author, or as studies of that middle world of which he is naturally and voluntarily a citizen."

46 ANON. Review of <u>The Wife of His Youth</u>. New York <u>Public Opinion</u> (14 June).
>With this volume Chesnutt proves his ability to interpret the characteristics of the black race. He delineates evenly the character traits common to all--warmheartedness, fidelity to those they love, and ingenious joy in simple things.

47   ANON. "Genius Among Colored Men." San Juan de Letrán
       (Mexico) The Two Republics (20 June).
          Favorable comment about The Conjure Woman and The Wife
       of His Youth, and a consideration of W. D. Howells as "the
       patron saint of the negro in his artistic endeavors."

48   ANON. Review of Frederick Douglass. Cincinnati Commercial
       Tribune (15 July).
          Chesnutt's estimate of Douglass is too lauditory. At
       times in his life, Douglass evinced "a certain lack in his
       nature which prevented him from being really great, and
       will, in time, relegate him to obscurity."

49   ANON. Review of The Wife of His Youth. Rochester Post Express
       (4 August).
          The stories are simply told and some of them are impres-
       sive. Nevertheless, they are often gloomy and discouraging
       to a fault. This is not an artistic problem though, and on
       that score Chesnutt succeeds.

50   ANON. "Interesting Biography of Frederick Douglass, the
       Negro." Chicago Times Herald (17 August).
          Chesnutt's account is entertaining and quite accurate.
       It is fortunate that he was chosen to write this biography,
       for, like Douglass, he has demonstrated to the world that
       black blood is not antagonistic to great achievement.

51   ANON. "The History of Shorthand Writing in North Carolina."
       State Normal and Industrial College, Greensboro, North
       Carolina, Magazine, 5 (October), 1–10.
          Chesnutt deserves "a place in the foremost row in short-
       hand work of native writers up to the end of the century."
       Chesnutt's accomplishments in this field are mentioned, and
       says Chesnutt has served two terms as president of the Ohio
       State Stenographers Association.

52   ANON. Untitled article. Current Literature, 29 (October),
       416.
          Biographical sketch and critical comment on "The
       Goophered Grapevine" and "The Wife of His Youth." The
       first of these is not at all inferior to the work of Joel
       Chandler Harris and Thomas Nelson Page. The second "touches
       a pathetic cord with rare dramatic ability."

53   ANON. Untitled article. Washington, D. C. Times (5 October).
          Comments on Chesnutt's three controversial articles
       titled "The Future American," published in the Boston
       Transcript in August and September. Says Chesnutt

1900

prophesied future racial amalgamation in American society;
reviewer supports Chesnutt.

54   ANON. "Short Hand in North Carolina." Charlotte (North
      Carolina) Observer (27 October).
          In an article about the history of shorthand in North
      Carolina, Chesnutt is mentioned as a prominent shorthand
      writer from that state.

55   ANON. Review of The House Behind the Cedars. Boston
      Transcript (31 October).
          Says book is rich in incident and suggestion. Not
      written from a "partisan point of view," it presents the
      problem faced by Rena and her brother objectively. The
      characters are well drawn. "This novel . . . with its
      strong conclusion--the race prejudice conquered late by
      love--may be taken as symbolical of what the author regards
      as the eventual solution of the race question."

56   ANON. "Charles W. Chesnutt's First Novel." Cleveland Plain
      Dealer (4 November).
          The House Behind the Cedars is a "strong novel" about
      the plight of the "white negro." "The temper of the work
      is admirable. There is no touch of bitterness, of passion,
      of prejudice. The case is presented with the impartiality
      of a judicial statement and left to the judgment of the
      great jury of readers."

57   ANON. "New Novel by Chestnutt [sic]." Chicago Times Herald
      (8 November).
          Review of The House Behind the Cedars. Chesnutt focuses
      on the plight of the mulatto. "He has opened up a new
      field of romance and reality, of which he writes with per-
      fect knowledge. . . . He is another brilliant example of
      the fact that there is no color line in literature."

58   ANON. "The House Behind the Cedars." New York Commercial
      (10 November).
          This is the story of the unhappy consequences of sexual
      relations between the two races. It has become a somewhat
      common theme. Howells dealt with it in an unsatisfactory
      manner. Chesnutt is evidently conscientious and sincere,
      and knows of what he writes, but his story is commonplace.

59   ANON. "Race Problems in a Novel." Chicago Tribune
      (10 November).
          This story, The House Behind the Cedars, "marshals
      forces about the walls of the white man's racial prejudice

like Joshua of old." But despite its moral posture, the
novel does not speak to the deception practiced by Rena and
her brother when they pass for white. "From the first the
story is well constructed, but neither in style nor in
characterization is there any freshness or originality."

60 ANON. "Mixture of Blood." Denver Times (11 November).
    Review of The House Behind the Cedars. This is a pathe-
tic tragedy which focuses on the "taint" of black blood.
Chesnutt handles well a theme which others have not. He is
forced to beg the question at the end when his heroine
dies. This makes the book more artistic, but one is left
wondering what would have happened if George Tryon had been
able to wed his love.

61 ANON. "The House Behind the Cedars." Boston Christian
    Register (15 November).
    "This book ought to attract many readers for its own
sake, and because of the light it throws upon a problem
second to none in its bearing upon American life. Whatever
may happen to the class he describes, Mr. Chesnutt has won
for himself a secure place in the literary world."

62 ANON. "An Issue in the Race Problem." Detroit Free Press
    (17 November).
    Review of The House Behind the Cedars. It is a novel of
purpose, and of more than ordinary merit. It shows that
neither law nor love can conquer racial prejudice. "Whether
we agree with all its arguments or not, it is easily the
most notable novel of the month."

63 ANON. "Not Rena's Secret Alone." Boston Times (18 November).
    Review of The House Behind the Cedars. The book is "a
capital story" and one which will "add considerably to the
already high reputation of its gifted author."

64 ANON. "The Race Problem in Romance." Philadelphia Times
    (18 November).
    Unlike Howells, who tried the same theme and did it un-
convincingly, Chesnutt deals with the theme of a love af-
fair between the races in a graceful, artistic, and convincing manner. In The House Behind the Cedars, Chesnutt
discusses "the whole race problem in its social aspects,
and it is handled with the clearest perceptions of what
really enters into it and what does not."

65 ANON. Review of The House Behind the Cedars. Cleveland
    World (18 November).

Chesnutt's use of the theme of the "color line" is not a new idea in fiction, and he does not use it well. Unlike W. D. Howells in "An Imperative Duty," Chesnutt permits the discovery of his heroine's black heritage to ruin her lover's regard for her. Actually, it was not Rena's "tainted blood" that caused her lover to reject her; "it was seeing her in the embrace of a black man, being forced to recognize a negro rival and finally seeing her come back into the neighborhood of his own aristocratic family as an avowed negress, teaching in a negro school." Thus the question of "tainted blood" is not the major factor, yet Chesnutt fails to recognize this.

66   ANON. Review of The House Behind the Cedars. Providence (Rhode Island) Journal (18 November).
In many ways this is the best thing Chesnutt has ever done. The situation is tragic, yet natural, and the story is told in a straightforward way.

67   ANON. Review of The House Behind the Cedars. Washington, D. C. Times (18 November).
This is an interesting novel for a number of reasons. It deals with the relationship between the mulatto and the white man, and its author belongs to the class from which he has drawn his material. The two strong points of the story are "the interpretation of character and the daring nature of the plot. The weak point is the style which is sometimes too conventional and conscious." There is an absence of artificiality in the construction of the novel.

68   ANON. Review of The House Behind the Cedars. Boston Journal (21 November).
"Mr. Chestnutt [sic] treats it [the theme of passing] courageously and with originality, setting aside the inherent sin in the deceit practiced and giving his attention to the white man who allows public opinion to daunt him."

69   ANON. Review of The House Behind the Cedars. Chicago Post (21 November).
This is a moving story due to the moderation used in its telling and the fact that the teller is himself in the position of those he writes about. The theme of the story is not new, but the story is told in a novel way. The major problem with the novel is that it is highly improbable that Rena's brother John would ever have been able to marry into the South Carolina gentry without giving a stricter account of his past.

70   ANON. "The House Behind the Cedars." Worcester (Massachu-
     setts) Spy (25 November).
         "The story is a very strong one. . . . Mr. Chesnutt has
     given it [the question of mulattos passing for white] most
     careful consideration in this dramatic story. The whole
     setting is typically southern, and the plot wholly within
     the range of probability."

71   ANON. Review of The House Behind the Cedars. Brooklyn
     Citizen (25 November).
         This book displays Chesnutt's lucid style and a "psycho-
     logical grasp and philosophical depth of understanding that
     indicate for the author a future of power." It will be
     appreciated by those who are sympathetic to the black race.

72   ANON. Review of The House Behind the Cedars. Burlington
     (Iowa) Hawk Eye (25 November).
         The novel shows how lives are wrecked by the inexcusable
     sin of mingling black and white blood. The story is well
     told.

73   ANON. Review of The House Behind the Cedars. Peoria
     (Illinois) Star (27 November).
         The novel is interesting, and even fascinating. This is
     largely due to the lucid, elegant, and natural style in
     which it is written. The characters, particularly the
     heroine, are well drawn. One cannot read the novel without
     coming to agree with Chesnutt that character is not de-
     pendent on race, and that individuals must be judged for
     themselves.

74   ANON. Review of The House Behind the Cedars. Boston Herald
     (29 November).
         "A southern story, told with no little power and close
     faithfulness to life. Its tragedy and pathos take strong
     hold upon the heart."

75   ANON. Review of The House Behind the Cedars. Chautauquan, 32
     (December), 334.
         This book is even better than the preceding two. Both
     major and minor characters are effectively portrayed and
     the plot is worked out with a mastery of the story-teller's
     art. In the story, Chesnutt neither moralizes or interro-
     gates. The story speaks to deep feelings.

76   ANON. Review of The House Behind the Cedars. Chicago Banker
     (December).

1900

Chesnutt, along with Booker T. Washington and Paul
Laurence Dunbar, is one of the most distinguished men of
his race. In this work, as in his former writings, Chesnutt deals with the plight of those who are neither white
nor black. "From the first the story is well constructed
and the style and characterization are fresh and original."

77 ANON. Review of The House Behind the Cedars. Critic, 37
    (December), 571.
        The first seven chapters are disappointing. The problem
    is stated in the eighth chapter, and from this point the
    action is engrossing. Chesnutt begs the question at the
    end, but he presents it with a vividness which leaves a
    logical conclusion in the reader's mind.

78 ANON. Review of The House Behind the Cedars. Southern
    Workman, 29 (December), 727.
        This is Chesnutt's most ambitious book. Rena's admirer,
    Frank, is the real hero of the story. Both blacks and
    whites are presented fairly.

79 ANON. Review of The House Behind the Cedars. Tuskeegee
    (Alabama) Student (December).
        Chesnutt is one of the first men to write sympathetically
    about the race question from both viewpoints. Thus his
    novel is one of the most vitally interesting ones that has
    been written dealing with the south. The story is simple,
    direct, and deals with present realities. The characters
    are strong and the plot moves well. This is an important
    book.

80 ANON. Review of The Wife of His Youth. New York Library
    Bulletin (December).
        Stories depicting the south are appearing with great
    frequency. "Of course the inferiority of the negro in the
    social scale must be admitted, but nevertheless he is an
    active factor in characteristic southern literature." Thus
    Chesnutt's stories come as "vivid sketches of the life and
    aims, good and bad, of the negro element in the south."

81 ANON. "Charles W. Chesnutt's New Story." Brooklyn Eagle
    (1 December).
        Reviews The House Behind the Cedars. "The conditions
    portrayed may be imagined, but it is a fair question
    whether they really could exist." Nevertheless, in this
    book Chesnutt has strengthened his already good reputation.
    "It is a strangely written story, and evidences all through
    its pages that the author is living, as he develops his

narrative, in situations that to his imagination are very
real."

82   ANON. Review of The House Behind the Cedars. Boston
     Universalist Leader (1 December).
          This is a "well sustained novel." "It is a pretty story
     told with dramatic power and presents clearly one of the
     great problems of the South with delicacy and fascinating
     interest. Seldom has there been sketched a finer charac-
     ter than 'Frank.'"

83   ANON. Review of The House Behind the Cedars. Lowell (Massa-
     chusetts) Morning Citizen (1 December).
          The book "gives a series of pictures of true southern
     life not to be met with in many books." It deals with a
     subject that is of importance to Americans, but the con-
     clusion of the tale reverses the usual order of things and
     allows a white man to avow his love for a black woman.
     Judge Straight is an especially striking character.

84   ANON. "Charles W. Chesnutt: A Cleveland Author and Talented
     Colored Man Who Is Winning Fame." Cleveland Leader
     (2 December).
          A biographical sketch placing Chesnutt in his Cleveland
     setting. Talks particularly of his legal work and his
     writing. Calls him a writer who has done more than any
     other to bring fame to Cleveland.

85   ANON. "A Negro's Book." Pittsburg Post (2 December).
          Review of The House Behind the Cedars. In this book
     "the whole tragedy of the race question in the South is
     given in a nutshell. The tragedy is portrayed as no one's
     fault in particular--yet it is inevitable from the start."
     The book has a clear style and a keen sense of dramatic
     effect.

86   ANON. Review of The House Behind the Cedars. Indianapolis
     News (8 December).
          "It illustrates how impossible it is in the environment
     with which the author deals to escape the heavy penalty of
     a heritage of negro blood." The story is effective and is
     told with considerable literary skill. It tells of deep
     tragedy and will produce feelings of more than mere inter-
     est in the reader.

87   ANON. Review of The House Behind the Cedars. San Francisco
     Chronicle (9 December).

1900

"It is a well told story without race offense or direct
moralizing." The book illustrates the social degradation
attached "to a taint of negro blood."

88   ANON. Review of The House Behind the Cedars. New York Press
     (12 December).
          This novel is better than Chesnutt's two previous books.
     Its literary workmanship is superb. Chesnutt's style is
     delicate, artistic, and strong.

89   ANON. "The House Behind the Cedars." Philadelphia Public
     Ledger (13 December).
          "The story calls out the strongest, most sympathetic
     protest against a condition irremediable for many years to
     come, if not forever. Mr. Chestnutt [sic] deals impartially
     with the problem and without rancor, suggesting no solution
     beyond the ancient, ever young law of Christ, and the sub-
     stitution of love for hate and cruel injustice."

90   ANON. "Mr. Chestnutt's [sic] Novel, 'The House Behind the
     Cedars.'" Boston Herald (15 December).
          Chesnutt is one of the first to write strongly and im-
     pressively of racial prejudice from both viewpoints. The
     novel is not only one of the books of the season, but one
     of the most "vitally interesting books touching upon racial
     distinctions in the south that we have ever read."

91   ANON. "An Unfortunate Heroine." New York Times Book Review
     (15 December), 931.
          Review of The House Behind the Cedars. The theme is the
     mistreatment of a beautiful and well-bred girl "on account
     of her negro origin." "The question of social equality is
     always a difficult one," though Chesnutt "presents in an
     interesting way the claims of our colored brethren, and
     the injustice done them."

92   ANON. Review of The House Behind the Cedars. New York Public
     Opinion (20 December).
          The importance of this book lies in the fact that it is
     written by a man who feels intensely about what he is
     writing. The book is the strongest when the cause of the
     blacks is argued. In other aspects, the book is not ex-
     cellent. The scenes are homely and crude. The dialogue
     is not dramatic, and the plot is weak.

93   ANON. Review of The House Behind the Cedars. Milwaukee
     Wisconsin (21 December).

The story tells of the pitiful condition of social relations in the south. "It is a sad and tragic tale, not always tenable as to its premises or plausible in situations. There are no episodes of remarkable character or strength to relieve the general mediocrity."

94 ANON. Review of The House Behind the Cedars. Boston Gazette (22 December).
The book is an extension of the concerns presented by Chesnutt in his first two books. It reveals a "growing breadth of conception and a firmness of touch." The story combines aspects of the romantic novel and a study of social conditions, but it goes beyond them to deal with "one of the greatest problems that concerns the future of our country."

95 ANON. "The House Behind the Cedars." Brooklyn Times (22 December).
This is a novel that displays craftsmanship. "The interest is sustained. . . . There is pathos and tragedy. . . . It is the old pitiable tale of the burden entailed upon the innocent . . . a story too common in the South." This novel presents a problem that needs a solution.

96 ANON. Review of The House Behind the Cedars. Newport (Rhode Island) Mercury (22 December).
This is Chesnutt's most important book to date. Chesnutt deals with his delicate theme fearlessly and vigorously. He paints an admirable picture of the Reconstruction south and his characterization is excellent. "As a story the book is more than interesting, it is enthralling."

97 ANON. Review of The House Behind the Cedars. Leavenworth (Kansas) Times (25 December).
It is a strong story of the "color line," involving "romance, very dramatic incidents and revelations of character." While its literary charm will attract readers, its deep significance will stir their profound feelings.

98 ANON. Review of The House Behind the Cedars. Philadelphia Friend (27 December).
This is one of Chesnutt's most ambitious stories. "The work is well done, the tale pathetic and tragic at the close, and yet we do not think he is as successful as in his shorter stories. As a literary worker he can be placed without hesitation by the side of Paul Laurence Dunbar and Professor DuBois."

1900

99   ANON. "Race Problem in Fiction." New York Evening Telegram
      (29 December).
           Review of The House Behind the Cedars. In this novel
      Chesnutt deals with a problem frequently discussed by
      novelists and sociologists, the proper social classifica-
      tion of those in whom the "taint" of black blood exists.
      In the story, Chesnutt "makes no plea for the introduction
      of the negro into the intimate society of the white, but
      thinks the general expulsion which generations of prejudice
      and the more or less natural social separation of the races"
      has produced "should not be extended to those who are Cau-
      casions in all but that single little clot of negro blood."

100   ANON. Review of The House Behind the Cedars. Boston Courier
      (29 December).
           In this book Chesnutt addresses himself to one of the
      pressing problems of the nation. Instead of directly sug-
      gesting a way to solve the problem, Chesnutt wisely contents
      himself with presenting the situation as it exists, which
      in itself will move the reader. Whether the book is con-
      sidered a plea or simply a story, it is excellent and
      interesting.

101   BANKS, NANCY HUSTON. Review of The Wife of His Youth.
      Bookman, 10 (February), 597-98.
           The title story of the book is "the first publication
      of a subtle psychological study of the negro's spiritual
      nature, the first revelation of those secret depths of the
      dusky soul which no white writer might hope to approach."
      The other stories are hardly worth mentioning, with the
      possible exception of "Uncle Wellington's Wives." These
      other stories show a lack of tact and good taste. Of
      these, "The Sheriff's Children" is perhaps the worst.

102   CRAWFORD, MARY CAROLINE. "The House Behind the Cedars."
      Boston Budget (25 November).
           Chesnutt is among the most successful of black writers.
      He is too much in earnest to dwell on the banjo-playing
      side of black life. In the novel he presents negroes who
      must be treated as human beings. The book offers no solu-
      tion to the problem it dramatizes; it only tells of the
      problem remarkably well.

103   HARRISON, JOHN LANGSTON. "Mr. Charles W. Chesnutt Has Done a
      Good Work For Those Races Allied by What Is Called 'Af-
      finity.'" Topeka (Kansas) Plaindealer (19 January).
           An appreciation of Chesnutt's work. Says that Chesnutt
      takes the situation of the black man and, "with keen

dramatic insight into the possibilities of this material, weaves stories of wonderful interest and great power from it." Nevertheless, behind the entertaining features of Chesnutt's stories there lurks a "well concealed appeal for a fairer . . . treatment of the colored race."

104 HOWELLS, WILLIAM DEAN. "Mr. Charles W. Chesnutt's Stories." Atlantic, 85 (May), 699-701.
A consideration of Chesnutt's writings, and particularly of The Wife of His Youth, The Conjure Woman, and Frederick Douglass. Calls the latter "a simple, solid, straight piece of work not remarkable above many other biographical studies by people entirely white." But says the volumes of fiction "are remarkable above many, above most short stories by people entirely white, and would be worthy of unusual notice if they were not the work of a man not entirely white." "It is not from their racial interest that we could first wish to speak of them, though that must have a very great and very just claim upon the critic. It is much more simply and directly, as works of art, that they make their appeal." While Paul Laurence Dunbar gave an interior view of the lyrical moods of black America, it remained for Chesnutt to show "those regions where the paler shades dwell as hopelessly, with relation to ourselves, as the blackest negro."

105 MABIE, HAMILTON W. "Two New Novelists." Outlook, 64 (24 February), 440-41.
A review of the work of Mary Johnston, and Chesnutt's books The Conjure Woman and The Wife of His Youth. Chesnutt's books are a contribution "to literature and to a knowledge of the negro race." They portray the black man in two tragic conditions, as a slave and as a free man. "It is part of the artistic value of these stories that this revelation is made incidentally and not with a didactic purpose."

106 WASHINGTON, BOOKER T. The Story of My Life and Work. Cincinnati, Ohio: W. H. Ferguson Co., p. 237.
Washington tells of his first meeting with Chesnutt before Chesnutt became well known, and of Chesnutt's knowledge of "the Northern darkey."

1901

1901 A   BOOKS - NONE

1901 B   SHORTER WRITINGS

1   ANON. Review of <u>The House Behind the Cedars</u>. Boston <u>World</u>
    (January).
         "It is a cruel story, but inevitable in our 'land of
    freedom' as nowhere else in the world. Rowena did well to
    die; for the black woman, however fair, the only safe
    'equality,' it seems, is in the grave."

2   ANON. Review of <u>The House Behind the Cedars</u>. <u>Literary World</u>,
    32 (1 January), 12.
         The tragedy of the book is the tragedy of color. "It
    is a cruel story, but inevitable in our 'land of equal
    freedom' as nowhere else in the world."

3   ANON. Review of <u>The House Behind the Cedars</u>. Toronto <u>Globe</u>
    (5 January).
         Chesnutt does not force his viewpoint, and is remarkably
    fair with the white man. The book is good, but might be
    improved. If, "instead of telling the story from the
    standpoint of a spectator, and with forced calm, he would,
    for instance, reveal the heart of the mother, or let
    Rowena speak, it is hard to see how he could fail to create
    a work of extraordinary dramatic intensity."

4   ANON. Review of <u>The House Behind the Cedars</u>. Washington,
    D. C. <u>Colored American</u> (5 January).
         The book shows a real picture of life in the south, and
    is a brilliant performance, "clear, to the point, keen in
    its interest, penetrating in its presentation of character."

5   ANON. Review of <u>The House Behind the Cedars</u>. Boston <u>Beacon</u>
    (12 January).
         Chesnutt wisely does not attempt to discuss the color
    problem; he merely presents it and the tale gains strength
    from this simplicity. However, the subject matter is a bit
    sombre. The race question is an important one, but it
    makes a lugubrious story that is painful for the reader.
    The aim of a novelist is not to make a reader suffer.

6   ANON. "A Daughter of Sorrow." San Francisco <u>Argonaut</u>
    (21 January).
         Review of <u>The House Behind the Cedars</u>. "This is a sad
    story, but not a strong one." The heroine is hardly real;
    one can feel little sympathy for her. The character of
    the brother is more believable.

7   ANON. Review of <u>The House Behind the Cedars</u>. St. Paul
     (Minnesota) <u>Pioneer Press</u> (3 February).
          The novel is strong, for Chesnutt understands the social
     conditions with which he is dealing too well to write a
     happy ending. At times, the book could easily fall into
     melodrama, but does not, and is instead marked by fine
     restraint.

8   ANON. "To Visit Home of His Youth." Cleveland <u>Leader</u>
     (6 February).
          Tells of a southern trip anticipated by Chesnutt. Com-
     ments on a house in Fayetteville, North Carolina, that was
     used in <u>The House Behind the Cedars</u>.

9   ANON. Review of <u>The House Behind the Cedars</u>. <u>Nation</u>, 72
     (28 February), 182.
          The novel appeals strongly to the emotions. Includes
     plot summary. Chesnutt shows frank recognition of racial
     differences, yet sees both black and white through a fine
     literary temperament, and "is not concerned to set one
     against the other either for praise or disparagement. He
     has an easy, educated way of telling a tale; and a special
     interest in the 'negro question' is not at all necessary
     for enjoying his work, or for deriving an aesthetic
     pleasure from his sincerity, simplicity, and restrained
     expression of deep feeling."

10   ANON. "<u>The House Behind the Cedars</u>." <u>Phonographic Magazine</u>
     (March), 55.
          In his first novel Chesnutt does not disappoint those
     who admired his short stories. <u>The House Behind the Cedars</u>
     "is of absorbing interest, and brings home to the reader
     a keen realization of the pathos and tragedy which too
     often fill the life of the colored man who has an in-
     heritance of white blood in his veins."

11   ANON. Review of <u>The House Behind the Cedars</u>. New York
     <u>Evening Post</u> (2 March).
          The tragedy of this book will not arouse the emotions
     of readers despite its strong literary presentation. Too
     many people will believe that Rena's lover is justified in
     breaking his engagement. To those who might be sympathetic,
     though, the novel presents a strong case. Chesnutt shows
     a recognition of racial differences and does not try to
     set one side against the other. An interest in the "Negro
     question" is not necessary for enjoying his work.

1901

12 ANON. Review of <u>The House Behind the Cedars</u>. Chicago <u>Advance</u>
    (7 March).
        The book is a powerful presentation of an old tragedy.
    "That slavery was as great a curse to the white man as to
    the black is shown most forcefully."

13 ANON. Review of <u>The House Behind the Cedars</u>. Philadelphia
    <u>Item</u> (8 March).
        The story deals with a problem that is too common in
    America. It is interesting as a novel and "tuitive" as
    a study of unhappy social conditions. It is realistic;
    scenes are vividly pictured, and characters well drawn.
    There are no exaggerations. The novel is "bright, thought-
    ful and entertaining."

14 ANON. Review of <u>The House Behind the Cedars</u>. Portland
    <u>Oregonian</u> (10 March).
        This is the most popular book of the 1900-1901 season.
    It has genuine story interest, dramatic intensity, and high
    literary quality. It also treats in a novel way one of the
    most important issues now facing the American people. No
    one else has ever treated the issue of mixture of blood so
    well as Chesnutt does.

15 ANON. "American Literature." <u>Saturday Review</u>, 91 (16 March),
    342.
        In a discussion of the widening range of American litera-
    ture, Chesnutt's <u>The House Behind the Cedars</u> is mentioned.
    It is a touch melodramatic, but Chesnutt writes with ad-
    mirable reserve. The story is not so important as "The
    Conjure Woman," "but it reports a bit of human history
    full of tragic significance."

16 ANON. "The House Behind the Cedars." New Haven (Connecticut)
    <u>Yale Courant</u> (16 March).
        The story is a "very pretty and pathetic romance. The
    interest is sustained throughout the book, and the critical
    situations are well planned and skillfully handled."

17 ANON. Review of <u>The House Behind the Cedars</u>. <u>Lakeside</u>
    <u>Magazine</u> (May), 53.
        The story is presented evenly and objectively. It shows
    the sorrows of the free blacks of mixed blood in a way that
    calls for sympathy. It is a powerful argument, replete
    with much "philosophical reasoning of a general sort."

18 ANON. Review of <u>The House Behind the Cedars</u>. <u>Minneapolis</u>
    <u>Magazine</u> (May), 21.

A decided addition to the literature on the south, the book is interesting as both a story and a study of social conditions. It was written to arouse sympathy for those of "mixed blood." This is not done by argument, but by presenting a realistic picture of their social and legal handicap.

19   ANON. "The House Behind the Cedars." Philadelphia <u>Conservator</u> (June).
Chesnutt is a good storyteller, but a better historian, for the best history is in the best novels. Chesnutt deals with the problems brought out in <u>The Souls of Black Folk</u>, but as a storyteller, he has the advantage of being able to present his case without polemical argument, in an honest and moving picture.

20   ANON. "Charles W. Chesnutt." Indiana <u>Freeman</u> (1 June).
Biographical sketch tracing the development of Chesnutt's writing. "Mr. Chesnutt's books, while couched in the form of entertaining fiction, are distinctly purpose writings, and he means for some time to come to devote himself to writing others along the line."

21   ANON. "Mr. Chesnutt at Work." Boston <u>Transcript</u> (4 September).
Account of an interview where Chesnutt speaks particularly of his methods of writing. "The March of Progress" and "The Wife of His Youth" are discussed, and public reaction to them. Mentions Chesnutt's views about the south, and his use of southern materials in his writings.

22   ANON. "Charles W. Chesnutt's Strong Novel: <u>The Marrow of Tradition</u>." Cleveland <u>Plain Dealer</u> (26 October).
"Upon a background of contemporary southern life Mr. Chesnutt has written a strong, virile and exciting novel. . . . Mr. Chesnutt has, in <u>The Marrow of Tradition</u>, far outstripped his earlier successes; he has written a story that will recall many points of <u>Uncle Tom's Cabin</u>, so great is its dramatic intensity, and so strong its appeal to popular sympathies."

23   ANON. "A Color Line Novel." New York <u>Commercial Advertiser</u> (26 October).
Review of <u>The Marrow of Tradition</u>. This novel, like <u>Uncle Tom's Cabin</u>, is unfortunately an outburst of pent up feelings. The story is too gloomy, and the reader is given the idea that the black man's position is hopeless. One becomes tired of seeing black characters who represent only fidelity and honor and white characters who are generally perjurers and murderers. The novel leaves a bitter taste.

1901

24 ANON. Review of <u>The Marrow of Tradition</u>. New York <u>Press</u>
    (2 November).
    The south has long been the stage for fateful drama.
    The scene that is now being played is the disenfranchise-
    ment of the black man, and it has its best presentation in
    this novel.

25 ANON. "From the Negro Side." Buffalo <u>Enquirer</u> (3 November).
    Review of <u>The Marrow of Tradition</u>. The book deserves
    the attention of all thinking people. None of Chesnutt's
    books approach this one for interest, dramatic treatment,
    or the importance of subject. In this modern <u>Uncle Tom's</u>
    <u>Cabin</u>, Chesnutt has presented the black side of a national
    problem. Events have proved that he is not overexag-
    gerating.

26 ANON. "The Marrow of Tradition." Springfield (Massachusetts)
    <u>Republican</u> (3 November).
    This is one of the strongest novels of recent years.
    "While viewing these scenes we stop and wonder if the
    whites are not degenerating to a level lower than that of
    the race they are persecuting." The book will exert an
    influence today like <u>Uncle Tom's Cabin</u> did in years past.

27 ANON. "The Marrow of Tradition." Brooklyn <u>Eagle</u>
    (9 November).
    The book cannot be measured by usual standards. It is
    a purpose novel, and thus the forces and problems that the
    book presents, rather than the story itself, make it im-
    portant. So judged, the book is strong and virile, even
    though it is often overdrawn and stereotyped.

28 ANON. Review of <u>The Marrow of Tradition</u>. Boston <u>Globe</u>
    (9 November).
    This timely story is as much a political document as a
    novel. It will attract wide and diverging opinions.

29 ANON. Review of <u>The Marrow of Tradition</u>. Washington, D. C.
    <u>Evening Star</u> (9 November).
    The novel presents "the race problem" in its ugliest
    shape. Given the present bitter resentment that is abroad
    regarding this issue, it should be questioned whether it
    is wise to stir up public sentiment about it, particularly
    in a novel where the writer's feelings are neither ob-
    literated nor skillfully hidden.

30 ANON. Review of <u>The Marrow of Tradition</u>. Portland <u>Oregonian</u>
    (13 November).

A strong and exciting novel. "With a clear conception
of the difficult problems which confront the South, and
yet with decided opinions where justice and wisdom lie,
Mr. Chesnutt has constructed a story which sweeps the
reader along to a conclusion that is satisfying."

31   ANON. Review of The Marrow of Tradition. Boston Commercial
       Bulletin (16 November).
           "Fiction has again given the best medium for presenting
       a great national problem. In Charles W. Chesnutt's The
       Marrow of Tradition he has presented the grave and almost
       overwhelming problem of negro rights with rare power of
       feeling and understanding."

32   ANON. Review of The Marrow of Tradition. Louisville Post
       (16 November).
           The style is direct, forcible and simple. The book is
       dramatic, if not poetic, and the characterization is
       strong. The last melodramatic chapter should have been
       omitted. However, this book should be read, and given a
       fair hearing in the south, as an example of the black side
       of an important national issue.

33   ANON. "The Marrow of Tradition." Portland (Maine) Advertiser
       (19 November).
           This is a novel of character rather than politics.
       Despite the tragedy in the novel it is not a story of
       gloom, for it is relieved by the story of an honest and
       successful love, and by "the conviction pervading the book
       that these dark ways lead toward a good issue." Reminds
       readers of Uncle Tom's Cabin.

34   ANON. "A Powerful Story." Chicago Tribune (20 November).
           The Marrow of Tradition is "a tale of great power. It
       is also one which appeals to every one in the present state
       of the negro, North and South. Mr. Chesnutt has colored
       blood in his veins."

35   ANON. Review of The Marrow of Tradition. St. Paul
       (Minnesota) Globe (20 November).
           This is a novel with a purpose, and that is to give
       blacks their political rights. But the treatment of this
       purpose is faulty. One side is presented as wholly good,
       the other wholly bad, and in the end the good are rewarded
       and the bad punished.

36   ANON. "The Marrow of Tradition." New York Age (21 December).
           This is the strongest piece of race fiction since Uncle
       Tom's Cabin. Chesnutt is a chief literary spokesman for

1901

blacks. He is the only southern fiction artist who views
things not from a black or white attitude, but from an
American one, with the exception of G. W. Cable. "As a
veracious story of the Wilmington revolution and massacre
The Marrow of Tradition will long occupy a place in American literature."

37   ANON. Review of The Marrow of Tradition. Troy (New York)
     Times (22 November).
          None of Chesnutt's former books is so commendable.
     Despite the fact that it will not please many, it is the
     highest type of realism. It is plausible and deals openly
     with race hatred and its consequences.

38   ANON. Review of The Marrow of Tradition. Brooklyn Times
     (23 November).
          This novel is less impersonal than its predecessors.
     Chesnutt presents a vivid, arresting picture of the south.
     "No unprejudiced reader, with actual knowledge, can fail to
     recognize the truthfulness of the picture, nor fail to be
     saddened by it."

39   ANON. Review of The Marrow of Tradition. Boston Herald
     (24 November).
          Chesnutt is a black advocate who writes well. He feels
     his position strongly and argues convincingly. His side of
     the case should be heard, and the blacks of this country
     are fortunate to have him as a spokesman. A better case
     would have been made, however, by fairly presenting both
     sides. As it is, Chesnutt paints the whites as animals.

40   ANON. Review of The Marrow of Tradition. Des Moines (Iowa)
     Leader (24 November).
          The story is characterized by the fire and passion of a
     fierce partisanship, a change from Chesnutt's earlier
     writings. "On the whole, Mr. Chesnutt does not seem to
     have been as happy in the writing of his new story as in
     The House Behind the Cedars."

41   ANON. Review of The Marrow of Tradition. Boston Christian
     Register (28 November).
          Thomas Nelson Page would have presented a different pic-
     ture, yet it could not be substituted for this one. Com-
     bining the two would make the most complete picture of a
     southern town during Reconstruction. From the point of
     view of his race, Chesnutt has written a convincing story
     that graphically portrays the problem of race relations.
     Chesnutt suggests no solution.

42   ANON. Review of The Marrow of Tradition. Chautauquan, 34
      (December), 327-28.
          A triumphant fulfillment of all that has been antici-
      pated for Chesnutt, the book presents a powerful indictment
      against the code of some Americans as practiced against
      others. The fearless portrayal of a mob's unreasoning
      passion makes this book a valuable contribution to the so-
      cial sciences. It gives the advocates of white supremacy
      a view of themselves as others see them.

43   ANON. Review of The Marrow of Tradition. Southern Workman,
      30 (December), 695-96.
          It is only fair that this view from the black standpoint
      should be made known. Not pleasant reading, the book is
      dramatic, vigorous, and vivid. Blacks are fortunate to
      have Chesnutt as a spokesman.

44   ANON. "The Marrow of Tradition." Colorado Springs Gazette
      (1 December).
          This novel will do more to create bitter discussion than
      to promulgate any practical solution. Chesnutt is too
      clearly prejudiced in this matter to write well, despite
      the fact that he knows the subject well.

45   ANON. Review of The House Behind the Cedars. New York
      Churchman (1 December).
          The book presents a fair recognition of the difficulties
      of the "race problem," and is full of passages that show it
      to be a thoughtful and observant study of southern life.
      But despite its promise, the book is not well done. "The
      plot is good and there is a just recognition of the demands
      imposed for working it out, but the author somehow fails
      to translate all this into action."

46   ANON. Review of The Marrow of Tradition. New York Christian
      Work (5 December).
          The author's aim is to show the oppression of the black
      man. The story is decidedly one-sided. It paints the
      whites as fiends. Southern whites may be prejudiced,
      overbearing, and hotheaded, but they are, from heredity,
      gentlemen. Uncle Tom's Cabin was a book for its times,
      but those times have passed.

47   ANON. "Mr. Chesnutt's Marrow of Tradition." New York Times
      Book Review (7 December), p. 938.
          The book is "skillfully written," even though some of
      the literary touches seem "too bitter or unfair." The
      main object of the book is to "exhibit the deterioration

1901

in character and conduct caused by the effort to oppress
the negro."

48 ANON. Review of The Marrow of Tradition. Kansas City
     (Missouri) Star (8 December).
        Like most books written with a purpose, its characters
     are types, not people. None of the excitement is really
     thrilling because it is too stock. Chesnutt's vision is so
     biased that his view of the subject is merely distorted.
     He argues social equality with the unfairness of a fanatic.

49 ANON. Review of The Marrow of Tradition. Rochester Post
     Express (14 December).
        "The novel is well written and interesting, but it has a
     serious blemish--it represents the negro characters as so
     superior to those of the white race that it loses force as
     a plea for equality."

50 ANON. "The Marrow of Tradition." Indianapolis Sentinel
     (15 December).
        At some points the book seems too bitter and unfair, but
     perhaps we are too close to judge. Chesnutt writes with
     bitter power, and if he does write with bias, perhaps it
     must be remembered that he feels the wrongs done his people
     keenly.

51 ANON. "The Marrow of Tradition." Atlanta Journal
     (19 December).
        This book will certainly arouse the emotions of south-
     erners who are unfortunate enough to run across it. Ches-
     nutt should publish his picture to show whether he is white
     or black. If he is black his work can be calmly dismissed.
     If he is white his work should be met with contempt.

52 ANON. Review of The Marrow of Tradition. Worcester
     (Massachusetts) Spy (22 December).
        This novel is "especially worthy." It is above the
     average of many southern novels, and is a book that will
     last. The most interesting character in the book is Dr.
     Miller.

53 ANON. "The Marrow of Tradition." London Inquirer
     (28 December).
        This book deals with the great skeleton in the American
     closet. It is an able exposition of the problem and a fair
     portrayal of things in the south. It is hoped that this
     book will produce an effect like that of Mrs. Stowe's.

54   ANON. "The Marrow of Tradition." New York <u>Town and Country</u>
    (28 December).
        "Mr. Chesnutt's work has the literary quality that was
    lacking with Mrs. Stowe, while the story is of the same
    evils brought (our shame be it said) up to date. It is a
    preachment that should work for much good."

55   ANON. "Mr. Chesnutt and the Negro Problem." Newark
    (New Jersey) <u>News</u> (29 December).
        Review of <u>The Marrow of Tradition</u>. Those who seek
    literary charm will be disappointed. Those who seek a
    dramatic presentation of black life will find their hopes
    realized. Chesnutt attempts to portray the situation dis-
    passionately, yet he is not entirely successful, for the
    book is written "from a negro point of view." No solution
    to the problem is offered, but perhaps that is wise.

56   CARY, ELISABETH L. "A New Element in Fiction." <u>Book Buyer</u>,
    23 (August), 26-28.
        A review of Chesnutt's <u>The Wife of His Youth</u>, <u>The House</u>
    <u>Behind the Cedars</u>, and <u>The Conjure Woman</u>, including a com-
    parison with the work of Paul Laurence Dunbar. Works of
    each merit attention because of "the circumstances of their
    authorship." Despite their dissimilarities, both writers
    have a "marked family resemblance in this extreme simpli-
    city, and in a certain homeliness of metaphor relieved at
    times by the quaintness of phraseology characteristic of
    the race." Chesnutt's three books are ethnological studies
    of extreme importance.

57   FITCH, GEORGE HAMLIN. Review of <u>The Marrow of Tradition</u>.
    San Francisco <u>Chronicle</u> (17 November).
        This is Chesnutt's best work. He has painted a graphic
    picture of social conditions in the south. In its stern
    unveiling of the sins of slavery the book is much like
    <u>Uncle Tom's Cabin</u>. It is amazing that given Chesnutt's
    knowledge of these conditions, he is so free of bitterness
    and prejudice.

58   GRIER, J. J. "The House Behind the Cedars." <u>Bookworm</u>
    (February), 72.
        Chesnutt has chosen poor material for this novel, but
    he puts the parts together well. The only purpose of the
    book seems to be to embellish the long discarded notion
    that the possibilities of the black man are only limited
    by the prejudicial attitude of the whites. The book argues
    racial inequality of an unusual kind. It presents the
    whites as inferior to blacks.

1901

59 HOWELLS, WILLIAM DEAN. "A Psychological Counter-Current in
      Recent Fiction." North American Review, 173 (December),
      872-88.
        The Marrow of Tradition loses quality in acquiring quan-
      tity, is less "simple" than Chesnutt's earlier works, "and
      therefore less excellent in manner." Yet "no one can fail
      to recognize in the writer a portent of the sort of negro
      equality against which no series of hangings and burnings
      will finally avail."

60 MILLER, CHARLES. "Cleveland Novelist Scores Big Success."
      Cleveland World (6 January).
        A biographical sketch focusing on Chesnutt's Cleveland
      connections, and calling him one of Cleveland's leaders.

61 WRIGHT, JOHN LIVINGSTON. "Charles W. Chesnutt: One of the
      Leading Novelists of the Race." Colored American Magazine,
      4 (December), 153-56.
        A biographical sketch and critical comment dealing with
      The Conjure Woman, The Wife of His Youth, and The House
      Behind the Cedars. Chesnutt is "the foremost colored novel-
      ist," and his work is particularly outstanding in two
      areas--in delineating the "mental anguish" and "heart rend-
      ing experiences" of those who "are too 'light' to be classed
      as black. Yet, not 'light' enough to be accepted as white,"
      and, in portraying negro superstitions and religious
      attitudes.

1902 A BOOKS - NONE

1902 B SHORTER WRITINGS

1 ANON. Review of The Marrow of Tradition. Bookman, 14
      (January), 533.
        Chesnutt is in earnest about all he writes. Despite the
      fact that there is much to criticize in this book, the
      pathos of it all makes one a bit blind to its faults.
      Though an exaggeration, it is "the cry of one human soul
      against the great injustice which he feels is being done
      his race."

2 ANON. Review of The Marrow of Tradition. Boston Universalist
      Leader (4 January).
        Chesnutt seems to assume that it is the rule for whites
      in the south to be habitually unjust to blacks. Chesnutt
      does not so much assert the goodness of the black race as
      denigrate the white. Such an accusation should not be
      spread about without careful consideration.

3   ANON. Review of <u>The Marrow of Tradition</u>. Wilmington (North
     Carolina) <u>Messenger</u> (7 January).
        Chesnutt has already written a lying account of what
     happened at Fayetteville, North Carolina, in which he
     maligned whites and gratified his own ego. Now Chesnutt
     has written a book of lies and slander that is teeming with
     fabrications and bitterness. Despite the fact that we have
     not seen the book, we have seen it reviewed and so know the
     truth of it. Chesnutt is particularly slanderous in the way
     he misrepresents the riot that took place in Wilmington
     (Wellington). In that case the blacks themselves brought
     it on.

4   ANON. Review of <u>The Marrow of Tradition</u>. New York <u>Herald and
     Presbyter</u> (8 January).
        A strong and intense story. It is made with great drama
     and will strongly appeal to popular sympathies. Some, not
     all, of the pages glow.

5   ANON. "Charles W. Chesnutt's <u>The Marrow of Tradition</u>."
     New York <u>Evening Telegram</u> (11 January).
        To readers who liked <u>Uncle Tom's Cabin</u> this novel will
     be appreciated, but to most southern readers it will seem
     outright folly. The arguments on each side are overweighted
     with considerations of pride and injury, personal vanity
     and indignity.

6   ANON. Review of <u>The Marrow of Tradition</u>. Seattle <u>Post
     Intelligence</u> (19 January).
        The book is a disappointment. Chesnutt takes a lot of
     good blacks and bad whites and puts them together in a way
     that points up their differences. The writer is so occupied
     with the moral issue that he forgets art.

7   ANON. Review of <u>The Marrow of Tradition</u>. <u>Literary World</u>, 33
     (1 February), 22.
        The novel has real power. The black man is here pre-
     sented by one of the race, and there is full insight and
     understanding. The most powerful scene is when the black
     doctor saves the life of Major Carteret's child.

8   ANON. Review of <u>The Marrow of Tradition</u>. Omaha (Nebraska)
     <u>World Herald</u> (14 February).
        This book will please northern readers and displease
     southern ones. As a novel it ranks high. As an advocate
     of negro rights it stands equally well and will doubtless
     be popular in the north even if it is not in the south.

1902

9   ANON. Review of The Marrow of Tradition. Independent, 54
      (March), 582.
        "A novel written apparently by a man with a racial
      grievance, and for the purpose of exposing conditions
      rather than to gratify any literary instinct in the author."
      This is a vigorous and vindictive novel. "Mr. Chesnutt
      will do well to remember that in order to make his enemy
      appear thoroughly despicable, he should be treated with a
      show of fairness instead of malignant hatred, which always
      excites sympathy."

10   ANON. Review of The Marrow of Tradition. Nation, 74
      (20 March), 232.
        This is a "purpose novel" written to make a statement
      about existing relations between blacks and whites in
      the south. The plot, characters, and situations are all
      designed with this end in view, and in his statement
      Chesnutt is "calm, acute and just." "While his novel is
      inferior to his short stories in form and method, it shows
      more vigorously than they do the capacity for cool obser-
      vation and reflection."

11   ANON. Review of The Marrow of Tradition. New York Evening
      Post (22 March).
        Plot, character and situation are all conceived to make
      a statement about social conditions. The characterization
      of both races is excellent, and the tone of the argument is
      admirable. "While this novel is inferior to Chesnutt's
      short stories in form and method, it shows more vigorously
      than they do the capacity for cool observation and
      reflection."

12   ANON. Review of The Marrow of Tradition. New York Christian
      Nation (26 March).
        This book does for today what Uncle Tom's Cabin did
      earlier. It vividly portrays the conditions surrounding
      the black man in the south, and the deplorable heartless-
      ness of the southerners. This book calls for sympathy for
      whites as well as blacks, "as they are both laboring under
      the load of injustice and suicidal prejudice."

13   ANON. Review of The Marrow of Tradition. Phonographic
      Magazine (April), 21.
        The story is one of absorbing interest and each character
      is followed with unflagging attention. It is written in
      clear, vigorous style, and though it contains no preaching,
      it has a moral. The oppression of the black race is harmful
      to not just them alone.

14   ANON. "Two Strong Men of the Race." Tuskegee Student
        (5 April).
            A biographical sketch calling Chesnutt "the leading and
        most successful novelist produced by the Negro in America."
        The Marrow of Tradition is his best work to date. Mentions
        that Chesnutt chooses his association with the black race.

15   ANON. Review of The Marrow of Tradition. Lowell (Massachu-
        setts) Daily Courier (23 April).
            This is the most important book on the "race question"
        since Uncle Tom's Cabin. Chesnutt should now be classed
        with Frederick Douglass and Booker T. Washington as de-
        fenders of his race. Despite some shortcomings, this is
        one of the pivotal books of this time.

16   ANON. "The Leopard's Spots." Southern Workman, 31 (May), 241.
            The Leopard's Spots, by Thomas Dixon, is compared to
        Chesnutt's The Marrow of Tradition. Both are bitter and
        one-sided. Unlike Washington's Up From Slavery, Chesnutt's
        book only portrays the bad side of southern whites.

17   ANON. "The Marrow of Tradition." Philadelphia Conservator
        (May).
            The black man can raise his position only if he does it
        for himself. Waiting for whites to do it will avail
        nothing. All whites are prejudiced with regard to blacks.
        Blacks only wish for a chance, not exclusive privileges,
        and they should have it.

18   ANON. "The Marrow of Tradition." New York Music and Stage
        (1 May).
            This is neither a good essay nor a good novel. The de-
        sire to make a moral point is too plain. Too many situa-
        tions are exaggerated. Chesnutt's feeling for his race
        ran away with him.

19   ANON. Review of The Marrow of Tradition. San Francisco
        Argonaut (5 May).
            To many this book will be a revelation as great as
        Uncle Tom's Cabin. Chesnutt's direct style presents strong
        characters who make the point of the novel well. This is
        especially true of the black surgeon.

20   ANON. Review of The Marrow of Tradition. Richmond (Virginia)
        News (24 September).
            This is an exasperating caricature of southern men and
        manners, to the disgust of the caricatured, who wish such
        writers would seek a more credible outlet for their

1902

    literary powers than to describe a locality they know
nothing about.

21   GIBSON, J. W. and W. H. CROGMAN. Progress of a Race, or The
Remarkable Advancement of the American Negro. Second edition, revised. Naperville, Illinois: J. L. Nichols and
Co., p. 348.
    A biographical sketch focusing on Chesnutt's legal work,
his work as a court reporter, and his writing.

22   PIPKIN, J. J. The Story of a Rising Race: The Negro in
Revelation, in History, and in Citizenship. St. Louis:
N. D. Thompson Publishing Co., pp. 122-25.
    A biographical sketch. Comments on the publication of
Chesnutt's books, and reprints a number of newspaper re-
views of The House Behind the Cedars.

1903 A BOOKS - NONE

1903 B SHORTER WRITINGS

1   ANON. "Cleveland Author Makes Addition to His Works."
Cleveland Leader (5 July).
    Comments on a recent article by Chesnutt in The Race
Problem, and on his future plans. Considers his views on
the "race problem," his literary style, and his achievements.

2   DuBOIS, W. E. B. "Possibilities of the Negro." Booklovers'
Magazine, 2 (July), 3-13.
    Chesnutt is presented as one of the ten eminent con-
temporary black men who are "the advance guard of the
race." His particular forte is the novel.

1905 A BOOKS - NONE

1905 B SHORTER WRITINGS

1   ANON. "Afro-Americans of Letters." Colored American Magazine,
8 (January), 4.
    Describes the accomplishments of Afro-American authors
whose works enjoy great sales. Chesnutt is a novelist
"pure and simple. He knows a good tale when he hears it;
he knows his subject always, and he knows how to dress it
up. Perhaps of what he writes is more of interest than
how he writes."

2   ANON. Untitled article. New York Age (20 July).
        Chesnutt will have a higher place in prose writing than
    Paul Laurence Dunbar will have in poetry because Chesnutt
    writes more as an American, while Dunbar portrays the
    American black. In The Marrow of Tradition, for example,
    it is not possible to tell from the book that the writer is
    black. This is also true of the work of Joel Chandler
    Harris.

3   ANON. Review of The Colonel's Dream. Cleveland World News
        (17 August).
        The forthcoming work is "an interesting contribution to
    the literature of the race problem." It is "singularly
    temperate in its dealing with these complex questions, but
    it presents the negro's side with all the force of quiet
    reality."

4   ANON. "Dream Doesn't Come True." New York Globe
        (9 September).
        The Colonel's Dream disappoints readers who have seen
    Chesnutt's earlier books. He has given a faithful picture
    of a small southern town, but the story is not strong.
    Chesnutt is more successful when drawing his principal
    characters from his own race.

5   ANON. Review of The Colonel's Dream. New York Evening Sun
        (9 September).
        The story is interesting but a little crude. The dia-
    logue is rhetorical and didactic, and the situations
    described by Chesnutt are not at all typical. Even if
    such conditions did exist, methods such as the Colonel's
    could never change them.

6   ANON. Review of The Colonel's Dream. Savannah (Georgia) News
        (10 September).
        "The story deals fairly and without prejudice, and is
    told in a refreshingly natural and attractive style. It
    cannot well be called a powerful story, but it is one that
    touches a sensitive cord in the heart."

7   ANON. Review of The Colonel's Dream. Chicago Record-Herald
        (15 September).
        This is a strong and quietly realistic tale. Chesnutt
    wisely allows most of the facts to speak for themselves,
    for he is a writer who presents both sides fairly. "Sel-
    dom, if ever, have the tragic and humorous elements of the
    dominant problems of the south been more movingly yet
    reasonably depicted than in this novel."

1905

8   ANON. "How Reform Failed in Clarendon." St. John (North
       Dakota) Telegraph (16 September).
          Review of The Colonel's Dream. "The story is rather
       slim, for it is only used as convenient medium in portrayal
       of a small, lazy, unreconstructed Virginia town." It does
       not compare to "The Wife of His Youth" and other stories by
       Chesnutt.

9   ANON. Review of The Colonel's Dream. Louisville Courier
       Journal (16 September).
          This story accurately depicts the "Old South" but tells
       nothing of the new, with its energy and drive. Colonel
       French is a northernized southerner who tries to solve the
       problems of the south and fails. He returns north where
       he should have stayed.

10   ANON. Review of The Colonel's Dream. New York Mail
       (16 September).
          Being a black, Chesnutt has an interesting view of the
       race problem. The Colonel's Dream is an antidote for The
       Clansman.

11   ANON. Review of The Colonel's Dream. Washington, D. C. Star
       (16 September).
          "This novel is presented in strong terms, but they are
       justified by the situation. It sets forth some of the
       reasons why the South has not progressed more rapidly than
       it has along the path of industrial development."

12   ANON. "The Shattered Arcadia." New York Times Book Review
       (16 September), p. 605.
          A review of The Colonel's Dream that primarily summar-
       izes the novel's plot. It is "rather thinly disguised as
       a novel" since it "sets forth conditions in certain South-
       ern States which affect the black man." "It must be
       acknowledged that the author does not spare the faults of
       the negro any more than he spares those of the white man--
       and in both cases many of his pictures are true."

13   ANON. Review of The Colonel's Dream. Augusta (Georgia)
       Chronicle (17 September).
          Chesnutt, like his main character, has become "hopeless
       in regard to the South." He should be ashamed to write
       such a pessimistic book. Indeed it looks as if this is
       really a thinly disguised northern attack on the south.
       Many of the situations which are portrayed are not typical.

14 ANON. Review of <u>The Colonel's Dream</u>. Buffalo <u>News</u>
(17 September).
The chief conflict in the book is between the ways of
modern business and old fashioned ways. This produces both
comedy and tragedy. It is a story that tells truly of
social and race conditions.

15 ANON. Review of <u>The Colonel's Dream</u>. Cleveland <u>World</u>
(18 September).
Chesnutt's usual high standards have not been maintained
in this novel. It is a monotonous recitation of one man's
views of the race situation. With this book, Chesnutt
descends to the level of Thomas Dixon. Why should Chesnutt
lower himself to quarrel with a simply lurid writer like
Dixon? <u>The Colonel's Dream</u> is not a novel. It is an
editorial.

16 ANON. Review of <u>The Colonel's Dream</u>. Brooklyn <u>Eagle</u>
(21 September).
This is an excellent picture of present black conditions
in the south, and would surprise many. Chesnutt writes
well and presents all the forces with which the black man
must struggle. It is a "very good novel."

17 ANON. Review of <u>The Colonel's Dream</u>. Chicago <u>Inter-Ocean</u>
(23 September).
"The story reads as if it might be a very truthful portrayal of conditions as they exist today in some parts of
the south." Although the story shows that the Colonel
fails due to the prejudices of lower and middle class
southerners, it also shows that the black man is far from
perfect.

18 ANON. Review of <u>The Colonel's Dream</u>. Detroit <u>Free Press</u>
(23 September).
"Mr. Chesnutt has made a vivid presentation of the
social and racial conditions prevailing in the south, turn-
ing the light strongly upon the limitations under which his
race suffers. He writes with an avowed purpose, and he
writes well."

19 ANON. Review of <u>The Colonel's Dream</u>. Indianapolis <u>Sentinel</u>
(23 September).
Reserved, quiet, and sincere, the book is more impressive and tasteful than Thomas Dixon's <u>The Leopard's Spots</u>
and <u>The Clansman</u>. It has a particularly strong ending,
"when the Colonel finds he must give up the beauty and
charm of the life he loves when he relinquishes his ambi-
tion to better it."

1905

20 ANON. Review of <u>The Colonel's Dream</u>. Nashville (Tennessee)
<u>Banner</u> (23 September).
The story is a kindly treatment of upper class southerners, but is libelous as to southern conditions in general,
and the stories of cruelty to blacks are simply false.
"The negro problem would likely be no problem, if it were
possible to stop its discussion, and it is greatly aggra-
vated by being made material for novels."

21 ANON. Review of <u>The Colonel's Dream</u>. Buffalo (New York)
<u>Courier</u> (24 September).
This is a "delightfully written story," with much human
interest. The conflict between modern ideas and the quaint
ways of the past is graphically portrayed. There is pathos,
comedy and tragedy, and the story deals with the race
problem in an intelligent and understanding manner.

22 ANON. Review of <u>The Colonel's Dream</u>. Cleveland <u>Plain Dealer</u>
(24 September).
This is more a picture of southern conditions than a
novel. The tone of the book is pessimistic, but not entirely without hope. Perhaps these conditions will change.

23 ANON. Review of <u>The Colonel's Dream</u>. Cleveland <u>Leader</u>
(28 September).
The best thing about the book is its moderation. Instead of growing hysterical about the wrongs done to his
race, Chesnutt simply tells his story and leaves the matter
of indignation up to the reader. This is a delightful con-
trast to Thomas Dixon. It is one of Chesnutt's strongest
books.

24 ANON. Review of <u>The Colonel's Dream</u>. Richmond (Virginia)
<u>Leader</u> (30 September).
It is hard for a southern reader to take up this kind
of a vital southern question when it is presented by a man
whose blood and rearing have made him alien to the aims and
ideals of the people he would educate. Chesnutt is a
talented writer, but he would do better to stick to the
simple tales often told by Paul Laurence Dunbar, rather
than talk of something he knows little about.

25 ANON. Review of <u>The Colonel's Dream</u>. Chicago <u>Post</u>
(30 September).
This is a story of a struggle of conviction against
prejudice and passion. Chesnutt has written a strong tale,
from his point of view, a story with much human interest.
Perhaps the book will help to solve the problem it presents
so well.

26   ANON. Review of <u>The Colonel's Dream</u>. Toledo <u>Blade</u>
(30 September).
"It is a sombre, almost tragic, tale, but it is one of
those books which brings the scenes it describes vividly
before the reader and leaves a clear understanding of the
situations."

27   ANON. Review of <u>The Colonel's Dream</u>. <u>Outlook</u>, 81
(30 September), 278.
Chesnutt is able to write very good short stories, but
in this novel he fails. This book is loosely constructed,
prolix, and dull. Some of the characters are well drawn,
and occasionally the dialogue is clever, but generally this
book is not as good as the two previous ones.

28   ANON. Review of <u>The Colonel's Dream</u>. Springfield (Massachusetts) <u>Republican</u> (1 October).
Thomas Dixon might well take a lesson from Chesnutt's
sobriety and poise. The novel could have been as sensa-
tional as the work of Charles Reade, but instead it is
reasonable and thus more convincing.

29   ANON. Review of <u>The Colonel's Dream</u>. <u>Independent</u>, 59
(5 October), 816–17.
This is an "up to the times" story, not at all a "before
the war" type. The style is easy, and the story does not
lack for incidents in which the relations between the races
are fully expressed.

30   ANON. Review of <u>The Colonel's Dream</u>. London <u>Daily Mail</u>
(5 October).
This book is slow, and deliberate enough to drag. It
is deadly serious, though, and will surprise English readers with the condition of American blacks.

31   ANON. Review of <u>The Colonel's Dream</u>. Liverpool (England)
<u>Courier</u> (6 October).
This is a readable and pleasantly written tale. Its
focus is the peonage system in the southern American
states. The absorption of so many American writers with
the problems of the south is not only instructive, but
ominous.

32   ANON. Review of <u>The Colonel's Dream</u>. Seattle (Washington)
<u>Post Intelligence</u> (7 October).
This story tells us of horrible conditions which are not
new to us. Nevertheless it tells of those conditions well.
The language and characters are appropriate, and both

1905

whites and blacks are treated fairly. This novel is a "photograph" of the south.

33   ANON. Review of The Colonel's Dream. Nashville (Tennessee) American (9 October).
       "The book is a bitter, passionate arraignment of the white people of the south in their treatment of the negro, and it does not contribute in any way to a solution of 'the problem.'"

34   ANON. Review of The Colonel's Dream. Philadelphia Enquirer (9 October).
       Chesnutt knows his subject but does not know how to develop it. There is no excuse for a story such as this unless it relates to existing conditions, and little can be learned today from the south in the eighties.

35   ANON. Review of The Colonel's Dream. Aberdeen (Scotland) Free Press (11 October).
       The state of things dealt with in the novel makes one wonder whether Lincoln really helped the slaves when he freed them. Chesnutt wishes to expose the evils of the southern system, and he does it well. This is a powerful story and makes a strong case against these lamentable and extraordinary abuses.

36   ANON. Review of The Colonel's Dream. London Morning Leader (11 October).
       "The incidents of the tale are crudely put together, the construction is often weak; but this is a book to get angry over, . . . with definite but well concealed purpose."

37   ANON. Review of The Colonel's Dream. Cleveland Gospel News (12 October).
       Chesnutt has written powerfully, although fairly, in the past, and he does so again. This book shows Chesnutt's characteristic sense of justice. Chesnutt has the strength of his convictions and, like the main character of the book, he too has a dream, a time when justice, peace and love will prevail.

38   ANON. Review of The Colonel's Dream. Denver Republican (15 October).
       This is a pleasant love story in which the interest is in the tale rather than in the problems presented. Troubles between whites and blacks are made secondary so that the reader can enjoy the story and not feel that his own notions have been handled roughly.

39   ANON. Review of The Colonel's Dream. San Francisco
      Chronicle (15 October).
          Chesnutt should confine himself to stories of the
      southern black. When he deals with whites a note of un-
      reality creeps in, in spite of his white blood. There is
      much strong writing in this book, but it is, finally,
      ineffective.

40   ANON. Review of The Colonel's Dream. Newcastle (England)
      Chronicle (16 October).
          Although Chesnutt sympathizes with the north, the case
      is never overstated. Though written with a purpose, the
      novel is still impressive, and is saved from being merely
      a social tract by its "love interest" and clever
      characterization.

41   ANON. Review of The Colonel's Dream. Southport (England)
      Visitor (24 October).
          This is a powerful novel which shows the social unre-
      generation of the American southern states. It is a second
      Uncle Tom's Cabin with none of the lurid melodrama of that
      book. The power of the storyteller and the reformer are
      so well blended as to disarm all criticism.

42   ANON. Review of The Colonel's Dream. Glasgow (Scotland)
      Herald (26 October).
          This is interesting beyond the average novel. It has as
      its purpose the attacking of the system of hired-out black
      labor, which produces scenes that are similar to those in
      Harriet Beecher Stowe's novel Uncle Tom's Cabin. Chesnutt
      is not sensational in his presentation, however, and the
      book gains from its simplicity and directness.

43   ANON. Review of The Colonel's Dream. Boston Herald
      (28 October).
          This is a strong arraignment of the south by one who can
      see both sides fairly and who understands the situation.
      It presents both whites and blacks fairly, and shows why
      the south has not progressed more rapidly.

44   ANON. Review of The Colonel's Dream. Knoxville (Tennessee)
      Sentinel (28 October).
          The story is written by one who is deeply prejudiced
      against southern laws and customs. It presents a distorted
      view of race conditions. The situations and people pre-
      sented in the book are unbelievable. Chesnutt should re-
      member the advantages given the black man by southern
      whites, not the least of which was educating and civilizing
      them away from the savages from which they sprang.

1905

45   ANON. Review of <u>The Colonel's Dream</u>. Charleston (South
        Carolina) <u>News</u> (29 October).
            This book deals with the old theme of race in the south,
        but it is handled by a writer with more tolerance than
        usual. There is little bitterness here. It is an honest
        attempt to understand the southern point of view.

46   ANON. Review of <u>The Colonel's Dream</u>. San Antonio <u>Express</u>
        (29 October).
            Chesnutt's prejudice, arising from his lack of sympathy,
        detracts from the message of this book. Both the political
        and sentimental parts of the book are unsatisfactory. Un-
        fortunately Chesnutt chooses to focus on conditions in the
        south which are not typical. Nothing is made of the "New
        South."

47   ANON. "Three American Novels." London <u>Times</u> (29 October).
            <u>The Colonel's Dream</u> is a serious work that describes
        with a "wealth of detail and no little pathos the attempt
        of a reformer, and the failure of his attempt, to grapple
        with the colour-problem in the Southern states of America."

48   ANON. Review of <u>The Colonel's Dream</u>. Louisville (Kentucky)
        <u>Post</u> (3 November).
            The approach of the author is moderate and manly. Al-
        though the picture is pessimistic, it is not overdrawn.
        The story does have its lighter side, and the author
        recognizes that there are signs of better things.

49   ANON. Review of <u>The Colonel's Dream</u>. London <u>Southern
        Guardian</u> (8 November).
            No novel of modern times has better directed our at-
        tention to the racial problem of the southern United States
        than has this one. Yet the purpose of the book is artfully
        concealed in a story that has many interesting features.

50   ANON. Review of <u>The Colonel's Dream</u>. London <u>Week Survey</u>
        (11 November).
            The book is interesting as a novel and yet unforgettable
        in its purpose. It attacks the lease system as the poison-
        ous growth it is, yet shows that the situation will not
        easily change. "The book is American, and upon English
        ears some of the Americanisms fall harshly, but it is well
        written with a distinct plot, clear characterization, and
        evenly-maintained interest."

51   ANON. Review of <u>The Colonel's Dream</u>. Los Angeles <u>Herald</u>
        (19 November).

That Chesnutt can write such an even-handed account of
this subject should be an example for white writers who
have also tried to exploit the same field.

52   ANON. Review of The Colonel's Dream. San Francisco Argonaut
      (20 November).
          This is a thoughtful and ably written story which shows
      the futility of grafting northern methods and ideals on
      southern minds and temperaments.

53   ANON. Review of The Colonel's Dream. Boston Transcript
      (21 November).
          The book is well-written and well-told. It could en-
      lighten the south, if they would listen. It is especially
      worthy of attention in these days of the intolerant Thomas
      Dixon.

54   ANON. Review of The Colonel's Dream. Chicago News
      (24 November).
          "The conditions [of the south] are set forth with
      clarity and force in a just and temperate all-round view
      truly remarkable."

55   ANON. Review of The Colonel's Dream. Atlanta Sunny South
      (25 November).
          Chesnutt writes with an ignorance of the inborn preju-
      dices of the south, although this is an entertaining tale.
      His story focuses on the old problem of the clash between
      northerner and southerner regarding the question of employ-
      ing blacks with whites in the south.

56   ANON. Review of The Colonel's Dream. St. Paul (Minnesota)
      Dispatch (30 November).
          All of Chesnutt's former work comes to fruition in The
      Colonel's Dream. The book is free from unnatural coloring,
      but still vividly depicts the unprogressiveness and back-
      wardness of the south. This will evoke serious concern.

57   ANON. Review of The Colonel's Dream. Southern Workman, 34
      (December), 691-92.
          "With dispassionate candor and without bitterness, the
      author depicts conditions in a provincial Southern town;
      shows the strength of long held convictions in battling
      against reforms, and the temptation that helplessness al-
      ways offers to brute force impelled by greed and ambition;
      and at the same time points out the path of the reformer,
      suggesting means for correcting present evils, and making
      clear the difficulties along the way."

1905

58   ANON. Review of <u>The Colonel's Dream</u>. Utica (New York)
     <u>Observer</u> (1 December).
          The novel's theme is the Colonel's attempt to reform the
     south. "Theoretically the schemes are not entirely wrong,
     but it is very evident that it is impossible to have them
     work out satisfactorily in real life."

59   ANON. Review of <u>The Colonel's Dream</u>. London <u>English Review</u>
     (2 December).
          Either as a political pamphlet or a novel this makes ex-
     citing reading. Although Chesnutt has a definite purpose
     in telling the story, he has not forgotten the novel which
     belongs to the better school of American writing.

60   ANON. Review of <u>The Colonel's Dream</u>. New York <u>Evening Mail</u>
     (2 December).
          The theme of a northern man having a difficult time ad-
     justing to the south is not a new one, but Chesnutt tells
     it with a new point of view, from the perspective of "an
     active sympathy with the colored race." This is Chesnutt's
     best story. "It is well knit and well told; it abounds
     with incident and gives us quick vivid gleams of thrilling
     little side stories all along."

61   ANON. Review of <u>The Colonel's Dream</u>. Yorkshire (England)
     <u>Observer</u> (15 December).
          "As a novel dealing with particular moral and economic
     questions it evades the pitfalls common to the class. Com-
     pact, uniform, smoothly and entertainingly written, the
     tone is one of studied moderation."

62   BRASCHER, NATHAN. Review of <u>The Colonel's Dream</u>. Cleveland
     <u>Journal</u> (9 December).
          This book has been written with remarkable fairness.
     Both black and white characters are presented honestly.
     Chesnutt writes with vigor and restraint. He is the
     leading author of his people.

63   DANIELS, JOHN. Review of <u>The Colonel's Dream</u>. <u>Alexander's</u>
     <u>Magazine</u>, 1 (15 October), 33-34.
          "Judging from the advance sheets of the volume this
     story is bound to be interesting. And if Mr. Chesnutt has
     written with his accustomed insight, it ought to contribute
     appreciably to the 'good end' of a proper understanding of
     the racial problem."

64   _____. Review of <u>The Colonel's Dream</u>. <u>Alexander's Magazine</u>,
     1 (December), 37-39.

The book is "an interesting study of unpleasant and de-
plorable conditions of the South." Chesnutt has the "art,
sympathies, feeling and knowledge" to write the great
American novel; "it only remains for the times and temper
of the South to wield its civil, political and social aspirations to the ideals of true Americanism."

65 MILLER, KELLY. "Achievements of the Negro Race." Voice of
the Negro, 2 (September), 612-18.
     Chesnutt mentioned as one of those whose achievement has
helped to raise the position and aspirations of blacks. He
is "among the foremost storytellers of the time." Includes
a brief biography.

66 SEIBEL, GEORGE. Review of The Colonel's Dream. Pittsburgh
Gazette (28 October).
     The book is an indirect answer to Thomas Dixon. This is
unfortunate, because controversy is not the function of
fiction and because Chesnutt cannot match Dixon's lurid
prose.

1906 A BOOKS - NONE

1906 B SHORTER WRITINGS

1   ANON. Review of The Colonel's Dream. Baltimore Herald
(2 January).
     "It is unfortunate that writers unsympathetic to the
South should take the common themes relating to that section and give them the common distortions. . . . The very
statement of the plot of the story condemns it to the class
of commonplace and cheap traductions [sic]. . . . If there
could be anything more flaccid and foolish and false than
this class of Southern fiction, it is to be hoped that the
American reading public will be saved the infliction."

2   ANON. Review of The Colonel's Dream. Athenaeum, 4081
(13 January), 43.
     As a piece of fiction this has a number of defects. The
narrative drags and some of the characterization is not
done well. The book is yet worth reading, for it is pic-
turesque, thoughtful, and sympathetic. The character of
Colonel French is particularly well done.

3   ANON. Review of The Colonel's Dream. Indianapolis News
(20 January).

1906

> A quiet but intense story, written by a man who feels
> what he writes about but resists the temptation to become a
> fanatic. The story is wonderfully interesting, and so full
> of information that it should be read by every student of
> economics and sociology in the country.

4   ANON. Review of The Colonel's Dream. Voice of the Negro, 3
     (February), 143.
>   The novel is "something more than a story. It is a psy-
>   chological study of the Southern man's attitude toward the
>   Negro." Chesnutt is "the most noted novelist of the race."

5   MERRIAM, GEORGE S. The Negro and the Nation: A History of
     American Slavery and Enfranchisement. New York: Henry
     Holt and Co., pp. 379, 384.
>   Chesnutt is mentioned as a contributor to the volume
>   The Negro Problem, and his article, "Disfranchisement," is
>   considered.

1907 A   BOOKS - NONE

1907 B   SHORTER WRITINGS

1   ROBINSON, VICTOR. "The Negro." Alexander's Magazine, 4
     (15 August), 209-10.
>   Chesnutt is mentioned as a prominent example of a suc-
>   cessful black, in an article lauding the achievements of
>   the race.

1908 A   BOOKS - NONE

1908 B   SHORTER WRITINGS

1   STONE, ALFRED HOLT. Studies in the American Race Problem.
     New York: Doubleday, Page, and Co., pp. 206, 428, 430.
>   Chesnutt is one of "those well known mulattos" whose
>   achievements are usually cited to show the achievements of
>   the black race. Actually, this merely clouds the issue
>   and makes it possible for the uninformed to say that the
>   black race is simply undeveloped, and not inferior. "The
>   Negro is one of the oldest races of which we have any
>   knowledge, and . . . its very failure to develop itself in
>   its own habitat, while the Caucasian, Mongolian, and others
>   have gone forward, is in itself sufficient proof of in-
>   feriority." Even the work of Chesnutt, "the most dis-
>   tinguished writer accredited to the Negro race," will not
>   change this fact.

1909 A BOOKS - NONE

1909 B SHORTER WRITINGS

1   WASHINGTON, BOOKER T. The Story of the Negro: The Rise of
     the Race from Slavery. Vol. 2. New York: Peter Smith,
     pp. 203, 289-90.
          Chesnutt is viewed as one of the most prominent novelists
     the race has produced. His southern heritage is discussed,
     and some of his stories are mentioned. The Marrow of Tradi-
     tion is the best description of the Wilmington, North Caro-
     lina, riot that has yet been written.

1910 A BOOKS - NONE

1910 B SHORTER WRITINGS

1   ANON. Review of The Wife of His Youth. Cincinnati Times-Star
     (27 March).
          The stories are accurate and show the art of a skilled
     story teller. "The Wife of His Youth" is the best story.
     Some of the other tales have the "slightly unpleasant sug-
     gestion of relations between black and white" that do not
     lend themselves to fictional treatment "but Mr. Chesnutt
     does evidently write alone to amuse."

2   BRAWLEY, BENJAMIN G. The Negro in Literature and Art.
     Atlanta: By the author, Atlanta Baptist College, pp. 21-28.
          A brief biographical sketch and a critical assessment of
     many of Chesnutt's books and stories. Chesnutt is "the
     foremost novelist and short story writer of the race."
     "The Bouquet" is Chesnutt's best short story, though "The
     Wife of His Youth" is more popular. The Colonel's Dream
     is his best novel.

3   HART, ALBERT BUSHNELL, The Southern South. New York: D.
     Appleton and Co., pp. 15, 325.
          Considers writings about the race question. Chesnutt
     has harshly criticized the separation of races. Perhaps
     this is because Chesnutt is "more Caucasian than African in
     his make-up," and consequently feels the distinction more
     keenly than most persons.

1913

1913 A BOOKS - NONE

1913 B SHORTER WRITINGS

  1   FERRIS, WILLIAM H. The African Abroad: or, His Evolution in
       Western Civilization. Vol. 1. New Haven, Connecticut:
       The Tuttle, Morehouse and Taylor Press, pp. 254, 271-73.
          The black race in America has produced only four writers
       of note--Chesnutt, Dunbar, Washington, DuBois--and none of
       them has been able to produce an "immortal" work. Chesnutt
       has written some "splendid" things, and is an interesting
       writer. "What he lacks is a quality that even few white
       writers possess, and that is the . . . ability to paint
       heroes and heroines in flesh and blood colors."

1916 A BOOKS - NONE

1916 B SHORTER WRITINGS

  1   BRAWLEY, BENJAMIN G. "The Negro in American Fiction," Dial,
       60 (11 May), 445-50.
          A brief survey of Chesnutt's writing. The Marrow of
       Tradition is not much more than a political tract. The
       Colonel's Dream has too much preaching in it, and The House
       Behind the Cedars is a "real" novel. Among Chesnutt's
       short stories, "The Bouquet" and "The Wife of His Youth"
       are powerful.

1918 A BOOKS - NONE

1918 B SHORTER WRITINGS

  1   BRAWLEY, BENJAMIN G. The Negro in Literature and Art.
       New York: Duffield and Co., pp. 9, 55, 76-81.
          A reworked version of the book published in 1910 by the
       author. Contains a brief biographical sketch and critical
       assessment of many of Chesnutt's short stories and books.
       "The Bouquet" is the best short story. Of the novels, The
       House Behind the Cedars is "commonly given first place."
       The Marrow of Tradition is perhaps too much a novel of
       purpose to satisfy the demands of art. Chesnutt is "the
       best known novelist and short story writer of the race."
       Revised edition of 1910.B2.

  2   REUTER, EDWARD BYRON. The Mulatto in the United States.
       Boston: Richard G. Badger, pp. 194-95, 198, 203, 208, 284.

A study of prominent black men who are mulatto, intended to determine whether exceptional men tend to be blacks or mulattos. The study concludes that more are mulattos. Chesnutt mentioned several times.

1919 A BOOKS - NONE

1919 B SHORTER WRITINGS

1   BRAWLEY, BENJAMIN G. A Short History of the American Negro.
    New York: The Macmillan Co., pp. 228, 239-43, 250.
        A biographical sketch and critical comment on Chesnutt's
    literature. "The Bouquet" is Chesnutt's best short story
    and The House Behind the Cedars is his best novel. "Mr.
    Chesnutt writes in simple, clear English, and works with a
    high sense of art. He is today one of the outstanding men
    of the race in literary achievement, and he deserves credit
    in treating in the guise of fiction the searching problems
    that one now meets in the life of the Negro of the South."

1921 A BOOKS - NONE

1921 B SHORTER WRITINGS

1   BRAWLEY, BENJAMIN G. A Social History of the American Negro.
    New York: The Macmillan Co., p. 312.
        Discusses mob violence in Wilmington, North Carolina, in
    1894. In The Marrow of Tradition, Chesnutt "has given a
    faithful portrayal of these disgraceful events, the
    Wellington of the story being Wilmington."

1924 A BOOKS - NONE

1924 B SHORTER WRITINGS

1   BRAITHWAITE, WILLIAM STANLEY. "The Negro in American
    Literature." Crisis, 28 (September), 204-210.
        Chesnutt was a fiction writer of high order. But he was
    "a story teller of genius transformed by racial earnestness
    into the novelist of talent. His natural gift would have
    found freer vent in a flow of stories like Bret Harte's
    to judge from the facility and power of his two volumes of
    short stories." Yet his "serious effort" was in the field
    of the novel, and he was partially successful in correcting
    the distortions of Reconstruction fiction. He was not as

1924

popular as Dunbar however, for his approach was too clearly
that of the realist.

2   DuBOIS, W. E. B. The Gift of Black Folk: Negroes in the
     Making of America. Boston: The Stratford Co., pp. 303,
     307.
          Chesnutt was a writer for the whole nation. By reading
     his works, many whites considered fictionally subjects
     that they would otherwise not have read about.

3   GAINES, FRANCIS PENDLETON. The Southern Plantation: A Study
     in the Development and the Accuracy of a Tradition.
     New York: Columbia University Press, pp. 87-88.
          In a survey of the development of the tradition of
     plantation writing both Chesnutt and Paul Laurence Dunbar
     are mentioned as black writers who have "contributed some
     rather artistic evaluation of plantation material." In
     particular, Chesnutt "handled his plantation material with
     considerable self-discipline."

4   WEATHERFORD, WILLIS D. The Negro From Africa to America.
     New York: George H. Doran Co., p. 406.
          Chesnutt is "the best novelist of the Negro race." His
     books are mentioned, and "his masterpiece," The House Be-
     hind the Cedars, is discussed.

1925 A BOOKS - NONE

1925 B SHORTER WRITINGS

1   DuBOIS, W. E. B. The Amenia Conference: An Historic Negro
     Gathering. Troutbeck Leaflets No. 8. Amenia, New York:
     Troutbeck Press.
          Report of a conference that met in 1916, in which
     Chesnutt participated.

2   VAN VECHTEN, CARL. Review of The New Negro. Edited by Alain
     Locke. New York Herald Tribune Book Review (20 December),
     pp. 5-7.
          Comments favorably on a mention of Chesnutt that appears
     in William Stanley Braithwaite's article, "The Negro in
     American Literature," included in The New Negro. Despite
     Chesnutt's faults, he can no longer be neglected, espe-
     cially by those who pretend to an interest in the striking
     literary figure of the race. See 1924.B1.

1926 A   BOOKS - NONE

1926 B   SHORTER WRITINGS

1   DOWD, JEROME. The Negro in American Life. New York: The
      Century Co., pp. 325, 507.
          A biographical sketch and critical comment on Chesnutt's
      books. Chesnutt "takes the highest rank among the Negroes"
      in novel writing. Like DuBois, Chesnutt "emphasizes politi-
      cal action and believes that everything is subordinate to
      the Negro's obtaining full civil rights."

2   NELSON, JOHN HERBERT. The Negro Character in American
      Literature. Lawrence, Kansas: University of Kansas Press,
      pp. 134, 135, 136.
          In prose fiction the American black has accomplished
      little. "Only one negro, in fact--Charles W. Chesnutt--can
      seriously lay claim to the title of novelist, and for the
      most part, Chesnutt was more propagandist than literary
      artist. He dissipated his energies in working for the
      social betterment of his people--an effort natural enough,
      and laudable, but nonetheless damaging to his literary ven-
      tures." Nowhere is this more evident than in The Marrow
      of Tradition.

1927 A   BOOKS - NONE

1927 B   SHORTER WRITINGS

1   REUTER, EDWARD BYRON. The American Race Problem: A Study of
      the Negro. New York: Thomas Y. Crowell Co., p. 286.
          "In fiction no American Negro has yet accomplished any-
      thing not surpassed by hundreds of other writers." Only
      the fiction of Chesnutt is worthy of mention at all.

2   SPINGARN, JOEL E. "Forward," in The Conjure Woman. Boston
      and New York: Houghton Mifflin Co., pp. v-vii.
          Chesnutt was the first black American novelist, and he
      is still the best. His stories are the first of a black
      American to really portray the fortunes of his race, and
      they are the first to give them real life. But The Conjure
      Woman is quite different from Chesnutt's later works. It
      is a folktale. In later books, Chesnutt leaves the world
      of fantasy and faces the reality of black life. In doing
      so, he was the first to grapple with the problems on the
      border line of color.

1927

3   VAN VECHTEN, CARL. "Introduction," in The Autobiography of
    an Ex-Colored Man, by James Weldon Johnson. New York:
    Alfred A. Knopf, p. vii.
        The House Behind the Cedars is "perhaps the first
    authentic study on the subject of passing."

1928 A   BOOKS - NONE

1928 B   SHORTER WRITINGS

1   ANON. "Author Wins Spingarn Medal." New York Times (14 June),
    p. 19.
        Notes the announcement of the award.

2   ANON. "Fittingly Bestowed." Cleveland Plain Dealer (15 June).
        Chesnutt will receive the Spingarn Medal for his "pio-
    neer work as a literary artist depicting the life and
    struggles of Americans of Negro descent, and for his long
    and useful career as a scholar, worker and freeman of one
    of America's greatest cities."

3   ANON. "A Native Clevelander Honored." Cleveland Gazette
    (16 June).
        A front-page article noting the award of the Spingarn
    Medal.

4   ANON. "Spingarn Medal." Cleveland Gazette (16 June).
        An announcement that the fourteenth annual Spingarn
    Medal, given by the N.A.A.C.P. each year "to the Afro-
    American male or female for most distinguished achievement,"
    will be given to Chesnutt. Includes a biographical sketch.

5   ANON. "Charles W. Chesnutt." Pittsburgh Courier (30 June).
        An article announcing a new novel by Chesnutt that was
    never published, but believed to be forthcoming. Quotes
    Chesnutt as saying: "The book is a novel dealing with
    Negro life of the present day, just as my former novels
    dealt with the same subject twenty-five years ago."

6   DuBOIS, W. E. B. "Postscript." Crisis, 35 (August), 275-76.
        The Spingarn Medal has been given to Chesnutt, and the
    medal "has seldom, if ever been more fittingly awarded."

7   HOWELLS, MILDRED, ed. Life in Letters of William Dean Howells.
    Vol. 2. New York: Doubleday, Doran, and Co., p. 149.
        In a letter to Henry B. Fuller, Howells discusses Ches-
    nutt's novel, The Marrow of Tradition. Howells says

Chesnutt writes of the situation with much bitterness. "But he is an artist almost of the first quality; as yet too literary, but promising things hereafter that will scarcely be equalled in our fiction. Good Lord! How such a Negro must hate us."

8 WOODSON, CARTER G., and CHARLES H. WESLEY. Negro Makers of History. Washington, D. C.: The Associated Publishers, pp. 310, 311.
    Chesnutt is mentioned as a writer of popular novels. A portrait is included.

9 WORK, MONROE NATHAN. A Bibliography of the Negro in Africa and America. New York: H. H. Wilson Co., pp. 463, 472.
    Chesnutt's five books are listed in sections dealing with "Books of Short Stories by Negro Authors," and "Novels by Negro Authors Treating Mainly of the Present."

1929 A BOOKS - NONE

1929 B SHORTER WRITINGS

1 ANON. "Negro Folk Tales." New York Times Book Review (3 March), p. 9.
    Reviews a reprinting of The Conjure Woman. Quotes with approval J. E. Spingarn's forward to the book, which calls Chesnutt "the first Negro novelist, and . . . still the best." The stories "have qualities of fear and wonder and whimsy, and deserve the immortality that is Uncle Remus's." See 1927.B2.

2 ANON. Review of The Conjure Woman. Philadelphia Public Ledger (16 February).
    Reviews a reissued edition. Chesnutt remains one of the "most considerable figures in Negro literature." The novel is "a folk tale of unquestioned charm."

3 ANON. Review of The Conjure Woman. Crisis, 36 (April), 125.
    Notes that The Conjure Woman has been reissued. Quotes from the forward by Joel Spingarn. All of Chesnutt's books should be issued in new editions. See 1927.B2.

4 CALVERTON, V. F., ed. Anthology of American Negro Literature. New York: Modern Library, p. 530.
    Includes a brief sketch of Chesnutt's life, and a list of his major works. See 1973.B2.

1929

5   DuBOIS, W. E. B. "The Browsing Reader." Crisis, 36 (March),
    125, 138.
        Notes the republication of The Conjure Woman, with a
    fine forward by Joel Spingarn. See 1927.B2.

1930 A BOOKS - NONE

1930 B SHORTER WRITINGS

1   CHAMBERLAIN, JOHN. "The Negro as Writer." Bookman, 70
    (February), 603-611.
        Black fiction in America begins with Chesnutt. Before
    he stopped writing "all the materials of the Negro novel
    and short story as a vehicle for dramatizing racial prob-
    lems had made their appearance." Although Chesnutt's best
    stories, "from a modern point of view," are his whimsical,
    poetic folktales that are found in his first volume of
    short stories, his novels display the high passions that
    followed the Civil War.

2   JOHNSON, JAMES WELDON. Black Manhattan. New York: Alfred A.
    Knopf, pp. 273, 275, 278.
        Chesnutt is an important black fiction writer at the
    turn of the century. Until the 1920's, "Negro writers had
    been less successful in fiction than in any other field
    they had tried." They had few things to their credit in
    this area. "One could look back to only one good writer
    of fiction, Charles W. Chesnutt."

3   KERLIN, ROBERT T. "A Decade of Negro Literature." Southern
    Workman, 59 (May), 226-29.
        Discussion of black writing from 1920 to 1930 in America.
    Chesnutt was the first black novelist to gain distinction
    before that time. The work of novelists in the 1920's is
    not inferior to that of Chesnutt.

1931 A BOOKS - NONE

1931 B SHORTER WRITINGS

1   LOGGINS, VERNON. The Negro Author in America: His Develop-
    ment to 1900. New York: Columbia University Press,
    pp. 256, 259, 270, 271, 310-13, 314, 315, 318-20, 324,
    326-31, 352, 353, 360, 398, 400, 403, 405, 440, 443,
    452-53.

Charles W. Chesnutt: A Reference Guide

A biographical sketch and critical commentary about
Chesnutt's stories, novels, and biography of Frederick
Douglass. The Conjure Woman is Chesnutt's best book, and
"positive evidence" that Negro literature was coming of age.
"Baxter's Procrustes" is Chesnutt's best work, and "perhaps
the best short story which any American Negro has as yet
written." Chesnutt's novels are not so strong artistically,
but they are "strong social studies presented undeniably
from the Negro's point of view."

1932 A BOOKS

1 GILL, ANDREW S. Remarks of Reverand Andrew S. Gill, Pastor,
Emanuel Episcopal Church, Cleveland, Ohio, at the Funeral
of Charles W. Chesnutt, Friday, November 18, 1932.
Cleveland: Wanement and Reilender.
   Chesnutt stood in "the front rank of the champions of
the people who have not always been given their brotherhood
rights."

1932 B SHORTER WRITINGS

1 ANON. "C. W. Chesnutt, Negro Author, Dies." New York Times
(16 November), p. 17.
   A biographical sketch commenting on Chesnutt's writings
and his books. He was "among the nation's leading literary
men."

2 ANON. "Charles W. Chesnutt." Publishers Weekly, 122
(26 November), 2040.
   Notes Chesnutt's death on November 15. Comments on his
literary accomplishments, his legal work, and his various
efforts on behalf of blacks.

3 BROWN, STERLING A. "In Memoriam: Charles W. Chesnutt."
Opportunity: Journal of Negro Life, 10 (December), 387.
   An obituary. Surveys Chesnutt's life and writings.
Concludes by quoting John Chamberlain about Chesnutt's
"ultimate position": "He pressed on to more tragic materials, and handled them as no white novelist could have
succeeded at the time in doing. And before he lapsed into
silence all the materials of the Negro novel and short
story as a vehicle for dramatizing racial problems had
made their appearance either explicitly or through adumbra-
tion in his work." See 1930.B1.

1932

4   LEWISOHN, LUDWIG. <u>Expression in America</u>. New York: Harper
       and Brothers, p. 355.
          "The mild croon of Paul Laurence Dunbar and the modest
       narrator's tone of Charles W. Chesnutt" were representative
       of a generation that "was soon superceded by others [like
       W. E. B. DuBois] who used a fierier tone and had a message
       of woe and rebellion."

1933 A   BOOKS - NONE

1933 B   SHORTER WRITINGS

1   ANON. "Charles Waddell Chesnutt." <u>Southern Workman</u>, 62
       (January), 41-43.
          An obituary focused on an historical and biographical
       sketch.

2   DONAHEY, MARY DICKERSON. "Noted Author in High Praise of
       C. W. Chesnutt." Chicago <u>Defender</u> (21 January).
          Discusses Mary Donahey's friendship with Chesnutt, and
       their meeting through the Tresart Club in Cleveland.

3   DuBOIS, W. E. B. "Postscript: Chesnutt." <u>Crisis</u>, 40
       (January), 20.
          A notice of Chesnutt's death, calling him "the dean of
       Negro literature." Considers his views regarding separa-
       tion of the races.

4   JANEWAY, W. RALPH. <u>A Selected List of Ohio Authors and Their
       Books</u>. Columbus, Ohio: Mimeographed Publications, p. 48.
          A list of books by Chesnutt.

1934 A   BOOKS - NONE

1934 B   SHORTER WRITINGS

1   BARTON, REBECCA CHALMERS. <u>Race Consciousness and the American
       Negro: A Study of the Correlation Between the Group Ex-
       perience and the Fiction of 1900-1930</u>. Copenhagen: Arnold
       Busck, pp. 75, 77, 79, 82, 86, 97, 109, 110, 116-18,
       122-28, 192-98.
          Chesnutt's work is compared to that of Paul Laurence
       Dunbar in its use of the plantation milieu and small south-
       ern town as setting. Also compares the view of the indi-
       vidual by the two writers, and the use of "emotional tones
       and colors."

2   WEATHERFORD, WILLIS D. and CHARLES S. JOHNSON. Race Relations:
     Adjustment of Whites and Negroes in the United States.
     Boston: D. C. Heath and Co., p. 482.
         "In Charles W. Chestnut [sic] we find a novelist of
     great ability. He was distinctly race-conscious; all his
     stories and novels center around the relation between the
     races." The House Behind the Cedars is Chesnutt's most
     powerful novel.

1935 A BOOKS - NONE

1935 B SHORTER WRITINGS

1   HATCHER, HARLAN. Creating the Modern American Novel.
     New York: Farrar, Rinehart, pp. 147, 150.
         Chesnutt is a precursor to the writers of the Harlem
     Renaissance. "The Sheriff's Children" was the first story
     to use a theme that was to become a common one.

1936 A BOOKS - NONE

1936 B SHORTER WRITINGS

1   WOODSON, CARTER G. The African Background Outlined: A Hand-
     book for the Study of the Negro. Washington, D. C.:
     Association for the Study of Negro Life and History, p. 400.
         Chesnutt shared the same purposes with a number of black
     writers who tried, often with "too much racial bias and
     little literary merit," to contradict the unfair image of
     blacks created by many white writers. However, his short
     stories and novels "reached a higher level" than did the
     work of most of his contemporaries.

1937 A BOOKS - NONE

1937 B SHORTER WRITINGS

1   BRAWLEY, BENJAMIN G. Negro Builders and Heroes. Chapel Hill:
     University of North Carolina Press, pp. 64, 234-35, 240.
         Chesnutt is primarily mentioned as a prominent black
     writer of prose at the turn of the century. Includes a
     biographical and critical sketch. "The Wife of His Youth"
     is one of his most notable short stories.

1937

2   BRAWLEY, BENJAMIN G. The Negro Genius; A New Appraisal of the
     Achievement of the American Negro in Literature and the
     Fine Arts. New York: Dodd, Mead and Co., pp. 3, 62,
     145-51, 224, 249.
          Chronological sketch of Chesnutt's life included in
     chapter titled "The Maturing of Negro Literature." Ches-
     nutt was the first black writer to give sustained treatment
     to customs, superstitions, and tales of black people.

3   BROWN, STERLING. The Negro in American Fiction. Washington,
     D. C.: The Associates in Negro Folk Education, pp. 78-82.
          A critical consideration of Chesnutt's books, placing
     him in the tradition of Reconstruction writers who pre-
     sented problems of the times. Chesnutt spoke out uncom-
     promisingly, but artistically, on black problems. The
     Conjure Woman recalls Joel Chandler Harris' stories, al-
     though the dialect is not so readable. It differs in that
     Uncle Julius tells his stories for personal gain. The Wife
     of His Youth "deals mainly with the problems of race." The
     House Behind the Cedars is also concerned with the color
     line, but in a somewhat conventional way. The Marrow of
     Tradition is less conventional, and despite its melodrama
     and poor plotting, has real power. The Colonel's Dream was
     the last novel. Generally, Chesnutt was overinclined to
     the melodramatic, to mistaken identity, to idealized and
     conventional characters. Yet he was aware of the sinister
     forces of Reconstruction, and his characters are nearer to
     truth than those of Page or Dixon. "Often pompous and
     roundabout, in the manner of the times, he nevertheless
     knew how to hold a reader's interest. . . . He knew a
     great deal, and all things considered, he told it well."
     Reprinted: 1968.B1.

4   BURRIS, ANDREW M. "American First Editions: Charles Waddell
     Chesnutt, 1858-1932." Publishers Weekly, 131 (15 May),
     2033.
          A listing of Chesnutt's published books, and of a few
     selected articles about him taken from Jacob Blanck's
     American First Editions. See 1942.B1.

1938 A BOOKS - NONE

1938 B SHORTER WRITINGS

1   MAYS, BENJAMIN E. The Negro's God as Reflected in His
     Literature. Boston: Chapman and Grimes, pp. 149-52.

Considers the image of God reflected in The House Behind
the Cedars. The novel "presents John Warwick and his sis-
ter Rena, both fair enough to pass over into the white race,
whose ideas of God are used to justify their pursuit of
different courses in life." "If the picture presented in
Chesnutt's [sic] novel is fairly representative of Negroes
who are fair enough to pass, it indicates that many Negroes
have passed over into the white race believing that God intended it, since he made them white." "The picture also
indicates . . . that many Negroes remain in the Negro race
because they feel it is God's will that they do so, and
that God lays upon them the responsibility of organizing
Negroes and working with them in the race's effort to
achieve larger privileges."

1939 A   BOOKS - NONE

1939 B   SHORTER WRITINGS

1   BROWN, STERLING A.   "The American Race Problem as Reflected in
     American Literature." Journal of Negro Education, 8
     (July), 275-90.
         Chesnutt was a "melodramatic" writer whose works "in-
     cluded many of the problems of the color line." "His
     social understanding should not be underestimated."

2   REDDING, J. SAUNDERS. To Make a Poet Black. Chapel Hill:
     University of North Carolina Press, pp. 39, 59, 68-77.
         A biographical and critical sketch which considers Ches-
     nutt's five books. Chesnutt was a "transitional figure"
     who was "the most solid representative of prose fiction
     that the Negro could boast before the 1920's." The Conjure
     Woman and The House Behind the Cedars are Chesnutt's best
     books. The Conjure Woman proved two important points.
     "It proved that the Negro could be made the subject of
     serious esthetic treatment without interference of propa-
     ganda; and it proved that the Negro artist could submerge
     himself objectively in his material." "For downright
     power, no novel of the Negro race quite equals The House
     Behind the Cedars." The Marrow of Tradition is Chesnutt's
     most faulty work. Here he "stumbled headlong into the
     dangers that had lurked for him in his earlier books." It
     is "definitely propaganda."

1941

1941 A BOOKS - NONE

1941 B SHORTER WRITINGS

    1   BROWN, STERLING, ARTHUR P. DAVIS and ULYSSES LEE, eds. The
          Negro Caravan. New York: The Dryden Press, pp. 13, 27-28.
            A general treatment of the development of the short
         story and novel by black authors. Chesnutt is the first
         black writer of short stories. Unlike Dunbar, Chesnutt's
         stories generally had deep implications. "No writer since
         Chesnutt has combined the deep appreciation of the folk
         Negro, of the transplanted urban Negro, and the foibles of
         the 'upper tenth' in the way that Chesnutt did." The Mar-
         row of Tradition is his best novel. In this novel, as in
         others, Chesnutt sometimes used melodramatic devices and
         stilted language, in the manner of the fiction of his time.
         However, he knew and portrayed social realities. A bio-
         graphical sketch is included.

    2   GLOSTER, HUGH M. "Charles W. Chesnutt: Pioneer in the Fic-
          tion of Negro Life." Phylon, 2 (First Quarter), 57-66.
            The Conjure Woman is a book whose stories "probe beneath
         the rose surface of the conventional plantation milieu."
         The Wife of His Youth "achieves artistic unity through the
         presentation in each story of a serious problem arising
         from the Negro's position as an oppressed group." The
         House Behind the Cedars is "Chesnutt's initial large-scale
         attempt to counteract the propaganda of the Negrophobic
         writers and to establish the Negro novel on a sound aes-
         thetic foundation." The Marrow of Tradition and The
         Colonel's Dream examine inter-racial issues.

1942 A BOOKS - NONE

1942 B SHORTER WRITINGS

    1   BLANCK, JACOB, ed. Merle Johnson's American First Editions.
          Fourth edition. New York: R. R. Bowker Co., p. 106.
            A bibliography of first editions of books by Chesnutt,
         and three articles by him. Some are annotated.

    2   BROWN, STERLING A. "The Negro Author and His Publisher."
          Negro Quarterly, 1 (Spring), 7-20.
            Chesnutt is usually considered to be one of the first
         professional black authors, yet his income from his highly
         praised books was insufficient for a livelihood. Further-
         more, like other black writers, he was often discriminated

against because of his race. For this reason his first
novel, The House Behind the Cedars, was put off in favor
of another book of conjure stories, and his publisher at
first demurred when asked to publicize Chesnutt's race.

3   KUNITZ, STANLEY, and HOWARD HAYCRAFT. Twentieth Century
     Authors: A Biographical Dictionary of Modern Literature.
     New York: H. W. Wilson Co., p. 274.
          A biographical sketch, and critical comment focused on
     The Conjure Woman. Quotes Benjamin Brawley extensively,
     from The Negro Genius, on Chesnutt's short stories. "The
     Conjure Woman showed that there had at last appeared among
     the Negro people a man who was able to write fiction with
     a firm sense of art." See 1937.B2.

1943 A   BOOKS - NONE

1943 B   SHORTER WRITINGS

1   GLOSTER, HUGH M. "The Negro in American Fiction . . . Sutton
     E. Griggs, Novelist of the New Negro." Phylon, 4 (Fourth
     Quarter), 335-45.
          Chesnutt's art is compared to that of Sutton Griggs.
     Although both use "the conventional subject matter of mis-
     cegenation, color prejudice, and racial oppression,"
     Griggs, unlike Chesnutt, recommends a better way of life.
     Also unlike Chesnutt, "Griggs tends to glorify black pig-
     mentation." Chesnutt, however, is superior to Griggs as
     an artist "in every way."

1944 A   BOOKS - NONE

1944 B   SHORTER WRITINGS

1   VAN DEUSEN, JOHN G. The Black Man in White America.
     Washington, D. C.: Associated Publishers, pp. 268, 270,
     278, 286.
          Chesnutt's fiction is briefly and favorably treated.
     "Negro fiction in America properly begins with Charles
     Waddell Chesnutt."

1945

1945 A BOOKS - NONE

1945 B SHORTER WRITINGS

  1   BULLOCK, PENELOPE. "The Mulatto in American Fiction."
      Phylon, 6 (First Quarter), 78-82.
           In a study of the portrayal of the mulatto in nineteenth
      century American fiction, Chesnutt is considered as "the
      outstanding delineator of the Negro-white offspring at the
      turn of the century." With A. W. Tourgée and George W.
      Cable, he brought to the portrayal of the problem "keen
      analysis, sympathetic interpretation, and sometimes
      literary artistry."

  2   DuBOIS, W. E. B. "The Winds of Time." Chicago Defender
      (3 March).
           Defends the use of the word "Negro." Through effort
      and struggle, by Chesnutt and others, "the word 'Negro' is
      no longer an epithet."

1946 A BOOKS - NONE

1946 B SHORTER WRITINGS

  1   DuBOIS, W. E. B. and GUY B. JOHNSON. Encyclopedia of the
      Negro: Preparatory Volume. Revised and enlarged edition.
      New York: Phelps-Stokes Fund, p. 60.
           Chesnutt is listed as a writer, and a brief list of
      secondary references is included.

  2   HUGHES, LANGSTON and MILTON MELTZER. A Pictorial History of
      the Negro in America. New York: Crown Publishers, p. 255.
           Chesnutt was "the outstanding Negro fiction writer of
      his time. His work focused on the tensions of Reconstruc-
      tion and the years that followed." Chesnutt's books are
      briefly noted.

1947 A BOOKS - NONE

1947 B SHORTER WRITINGS

  1   FRANKLIN, JOHN HOPE. From Slavery to Freedom: A History of
      Negro Americans. New York: Alfred A. Knopf, pp. 301, 302.
           Chesnutt mentioned primarily as the "writer who made the
      greatest impression" during the period at the turn of the
      century.

1948 A   BOOKS - NONE

1948 B   SHORTER WRITINGS

1   BENÉT, WILLIAM ROSE. The Reader's Encyclopedia. New York:
     Thomas Y. Crowell Co., p. 191.
         A biographical sketch. Chesnutt is sometimes called the
     first black novelist. His first book centers on a charac-
     ter much like Uncle Remus. His later books deal with race
     prejudice.

2   BONTEMPS, ARNA. Story of the Negro. New York: Alfred A.
     Knopf, pp. 196-97.
         A book for juvenile readers. Mentions Chesnutt as a
     black attorney and writer of books that "proved his ability
     to tell stories well and to win the respect of critical
     readers."

3   CHANDLER, G. LEWIS. "Coming of Age: A Note on American Negro
     Novelists." Phylon, 9 (First Quarter), 25-29.
         Considers the development of the black novel before
     Richard Wright's Native Son; The Marrow of Tradition and
     The House Behind the Cedars are mentioned with others as
     typical of the early black novel. They are "plastered with
     propaganda, with the urge to protest and vindicate. In an
     attempt to establish their theses, these authors in true
     propaganda technique invariably load the dice; and without
     artistic symmetry or restraint, they tend to oversimplify
     and slice thinly a complex situation, all to fit a pre-
     formed thesis." Thus, these novels are "conspicuously
     lacking in perspective, range, balance, logic, objectivity."

4   GLOSTER, HUGH M. Negro Voices in American Fiction. Chapel
     Hill: University of North Carolina Press, pp. 23-24, 34-46,
     54, 57, 66-67, 72, 82, 90, 98, 99, 100, 110, 112, 138,
     149-50, 179, 261-62.
         Chesnutt is "a gifted novelist" and "one of the signifi-
     cant figures in American Negro Literature." The Conjure
     Woman, although suggestive of Joel Chandler Harris's work,
     objectively probes beneath the surface of the conventional
     plantation setting. The Wife of His Youth, focusing on
     the problems of near-whites, "achieves artistic unity
     through the presentation in each story of a serious problem
     arising from the Negro's position in the American social
     order." The House Behind the Cedars, "essentially a story
     of crossing the color line," is Chesnutt's initial large-
     scale attempt to "counteract the propaganda of race-baiting
     writers and to establish the novel of Negro life on a sound

1948

esthetic foundation." Both this novel and Chesnutt's next
one, The Marrow of Tradition, are gloomy views of race relations offering no panacea for the ills that are exposed.
Chesnutt's final novel, The Colonel's Dream, shows the conflict between entrenched prejudice and idealistic reform
in the south.

5   GLOSTER, HUGH M.   "The Negro Writer and the Southern Scene."
     Southern Packet, 4 (January), 1-3.
          Chesnutt was a skillful black writer who defended the
     black man, described his difficulties, and asserted his
     right to democracy. The Conjure Woman perpetuates planta-
     tion sentimentalities but his other books stress the con-
     sequences of prejudice.

6   WALSER, RICHARD, ed.   North Carolina in the Short Story.
     Chapel Hill: University of North Carolina Press, pp. 76-77.
          A biographical sketch introducing a short story by Ches-
     nutt. He was the "first Negro writer to employ the short
     story as a serious medium of artistic expression." The
     stories in The Conjure Woman are his best remembered, be-
     cause they "are told from the viewpoint of the white man
     who has respect and toleration for the picturesque Negro
     slave."

1949 A   BOOKS - NONE

1949 B   SHORTER WRITINGS

1   FRAZIER, E. FRANKLIN.   The Negro in the United States.
     New York: The Macmillan Co., p. 505.
          A brief biographical and critical sketch. Chesnutt is
     one of the two outstanding black literary figures at the
     turn of the century. "Baxter's Procrustes" is his best
     story. The Conjure Woman set the level of achievement for
     his books. "If Chestnutt [sic] had written only these two
     pieces, he would have a distinguished place in the history
     of the literary development of the Negro."

2   OTTLEY, ROI.   Black Odyssey: The Story of the Negro in
     America. London: John Murray, pp. 201, 251.
          Chesnutt mentioned as a prominent black writer who had
     come from the "black bourgeoisie."

3   PARKER, JOHN W.   "Chesnutt as a Southern Town Remembers Him."
     Crisis, 56 (July), 205-206, 221.

A biographical sketch drawing on the memories of Chesnutt's family and acquaintances in Fayetteville, North Carolina.

4   REDDING, J. SAUNDERS. "American Negro Literature." _American Scholar_, 18 (Spring), 137–48.
By 1906, when he stopped writing, Chesnutt was the best black writer of prose fiction. At the beginning of his writing career, Chesnutt's race was kept a secret since "a literary work by an American of acknowledged color was a doubtful experiment." Two of his later books, _The Marrow of Tradition_ and _The Colonel's Dream_, did not pay the cost of their printing, for they were too honest, and were propaganda. Audiences were indifferent because these books went against the concepts that were the props of the dialect tradition. If Chesnutt had not had an established reputation as a short story writer, his novels would probably never have been published. His short stories are his best works.

1950 A   BOOKS – NONE

1950 B   SHORTER WRITINGS

1   BROWN, STERLING A. "Negro Folk Expression." _Phylon_, 11 (Fourth Quarter), 318–27.
Chesnutt mentioned as a prominent black writer who used black folk tales and beliefs in _The Conjure Woman_.

2   COTHRAN, TILMAN C. "White Stereotypes in Fiction by Negroes." _Phylon_, 11 (Third Quarter), 252–56.
In a study of "the content and range of the stereotyped conceptions of white people set forth in fiction by Negro writers," Chesnutt's books are mentioned frequently with regard to black stereotypes about white morals, white inferiority, and the issue of intermarriage between the races.

3   DREER, HERMAN. _American Literature by Negro Authors_. New York: The Macmillan Co., pp. 229–30.
A biographical sketch introducing a short story by Chesnutt. Chesnutt is the first black writer to be aware of the techniques of the novel and short story as genuine art. His short stories and novels are "comparable to the works of other writers of American fiction."

1950

4   REDDING, J. SAUNDERS. They Came in Chains: Americans From
    Africa. Philadelphia: J. B. Lippincott Co., pp. 206, 210.
        Chesnutt mentioned as a distinguished black writer whose
    novels were "too obviously the work of a Negro, and they
    were ignored. They did not fit into the frame of the
    expected."

5   _____. "The Negro Writer--Shadow and Substance." Phylon, 11
    (Fourth Quarter), 371-73.
        Chesnutt and Sutton Griggs mentioned as two of the few
    early black writers who tried to "deal sincerely, and/or
    profoundly, with Negro life. When they did, or tried to,
    they were rejected."

1951 A   BOOKS - NONE

1951 B   SHORTER WRITINGS

1   QUINN, ARTHUR HOBSON. The Literature of the American People:
    An Historical and Critical Survey. New York: Appleton-
    Century-Crofts, p. 919.
        Literature by American blacks was not considered a good
    risk by publishing houses before Chesnutt's work. The
    eventual publication of his "problem novels" was made
    possible only by the fact that Chesnutt had first attained
    a reputation as a short story writer before the secret of
    his race was disclosed. His short stories were his best
    work.

1952 A   BOOKS

1   CHESNUTT, HELEN M. Charles Waddell Chesnutt: Pioneer of the
    Color Line. Chapel Hill: University of North Carolina
    Press, 324 pp.
        A primarily historical biography written by Chesnutt's
    daughter. Makes extensive use of the papers, manuscripts,
    and correspondence of Chesnutt, now in the Fisk University
    library. Includes little critical analysis of Chesnutt's
    works, but focuses on material from letters, diaries, and
    other primary sources. Neither reference citations nor a
    bibliography is included.

Charles W. Chesnutt: A Reference Guide

1952 B SHORTER WRITINGS

1 BONTEMPS, ARNA. "Chesnutt Papers Go to Fisk." Library
   Journal, 77 (August), 1288-1289.
   Comments on Chesnutt's place in American letters, and
   on his daughter's gift of Chesnutt's manuscripts, papers,
   and memorabilia to Fisk University, Nashville. Briefly
   mentions some items in the collection, and explains their
   value.

2 BROOKS, VAN WYCK. The Confident Years 1885-1915. New York:
   E. P. Dutton and Co., pp. 545-46.
   Chesnutt and Paul Laurence Dunbar were precursors of
   the writers of the Harlem Renaissance, though their work
   was outmoded by that time. Chesnutt's stories were
   "gathered from former slaves," but "related from the point
   of view of whites, in the manner of Thomas Nelson Page and
   Joel Chandler Harris." A "modern phase" of Chesnutt's later
   writing dealt more firmly with the problems of color.

3 DAVIS, ARTHUR P. Review of Charles Waddell Chesnutt: Pioneer
   of the Color Line, by Helen M. Chesnutt. Journal of Negro
   History, 37 (October), 470-72.
   The biography is "refreshing and fascinating," and provides "a vivid picture" of upper class Negro life during
   the late nineteenth and early twentieth centuries. The
   life of Chesnutt is told through journals and letters,
   skillfully selected and edited. A negligible fault is the
   author's slight tendency to idealize her father. See
   1952.A1.

4 Joint Committee of the North Carolina English Teachers Association and the North Carolina Library Association. North
   Carolina Authors: A Selective Handbook. Chapel Hill:
   University of North Carolina Library, pp. 19-20.
   A biographical and critical comment. Chesnutt is "the
   first North Carolina writer to make use of racial tradi-
   tions and superstitions." He dared to tell "(1) the
   miseries of slavery, (2) the basic interracial and intra-
   racial problems in the misadministration of the Reconstruction, and (3) discrimination, segregation, and miscegina-
   tion as prime factors in the Race Problem since Reconstruction."

5 MOON, BUCKLIN. "Fighter Against Bias." New York Times
   (29 June), p. 4.
   Review of Charles Waddell Chesnutt: Pioneer of the
   Color Line. The book is a "warm and intimate family

1952

portrait told with tenderness and honesty." Chesnutt was the first black writer to receive any real critical acclaim. His work employed many themes that would not be used by other writers until much later. See 1952.A1.

1953 A BOOKS - NONE

1953 B SHORTER WRITINGS

1   AMES, RUSSELL. "Social Realism in Charles W. Chesnutt," Phylon, 14 (Second Quarter), 199-206.
        Chesnutt is "the first distinguished American Negro author of short stories and novels." At the time he wrote, Chesnutt's "main theme could not be liberation but had to be resistence and retreat. His protagonists could not be very large, victorious, or forward-moving." His "method was to disarm his readers with conventional scenes and seeming stereotypes . . . and then in lightening flashes to reveal the underlying facts of injustice and rebellion." Discusses Chesnutt's "objectivity," and compares his view of the south and its history to that of Faulkner. "If . . . one considers most fiction today, and typically the fiction of Faulkner, to be decadent, both in what it says and in the garbled way in which it is said, then the social realism of Chesnutt represents a peak from which our fiction has declined." Rather than being "decadent," the writing of Chesnutt "is propaganda for reason, for the understanding of society, for the development of human beings. It is artistic in the large, sound meanings of the term." In creating "real social beings tied to a particular social fabric," the "clarity and liveliness of characterization" in his work is "remarkable," and far better than that of Hemingway, Dos Passos, Faulkner, Joyce, and "most of Steinbeck," which has an "empty modern sense." Biographical information included. Reprinted: 1970.B8.

2   HUGHES, CARL MILTON. The Negro Novelist; A Discussion of the Writings of American Negro Novelists 1940-1950. New York: The Citadel Press, pp. 34, 39, 42, 43, 44, 131, 138, 196, 235.
        Chesnutt was part of "a group of Negro writers, guided by a sense of reform and protest based on moral compunctions, who wrote competent novels" at the beginning of the nineteenth century. The House Behind the Cedars pioneered the portrayal of race differences. It is a "true work of art."

1954

3   SILLEN, SAMUEL. "Charles W. Chesnutt: A Pioneer Negro
      Novelist." Masses and Mainstream, 6 (February), 8-14.
          A biographical and critical sketch focusing on Chesnutt
      as "a sharp-eyed, militant and highly talented critic of
      the whole abominable system of Negro oppression in this
      country." The Marrow of Tradition is particularly dis-
      cussed and is called "an American classic."

1954 A   BOOKS

1   FREENEY, MILDRED and MARY T. HENRY. A List of Manuscripts,
      Published Works, and Related Items in the Charles Waddell
      Chesnutt Collection of the Erastus Milo Cravath Memorial
      Library. Nashville: Fisk University Library.
          The collection contains manuscripts of Chesnutt's
      articles, books--some of which are unpublished--a play,
      poems, short stories, speeches, ten journals and scrap-
      books, and considerable correspondence. See 1954.B1;
      1973.A1.

1954 B   SHORTER WRITINGS

1   BONTEMPS, ARNA. "Introduction" to A List of Manuscripts,
      Published Works, and Related Items in the Charles Waddell
      Chesnutt Collection of the Erastus Milo Cravath Memorial
      Library, by Mildred Freeney and Mary T. Henry. Nashville:
      Fisk University Library, pp. 3-4.
          Chesnutt was the first black American writer to receive
      serious attention for his stories and novels. He was a
      "literary disciple" of George Washington Cable. Describes
      the contents of the collection, and comments on its dona-
      tion by Chesnutt's daughter. See 1954.A1; 1973.A1.

2   LEARY, LEWIS. Articles on American Literature 1900-1950.
      Durham, North Carolina: Duke University Press, p. 42.
          A list that includes primary and secondary works. In-
      cludes three articles related to Chesnutt, two about him
      and one by him.

3   LEFLER, HUGH TALMAGE, and ALBERT RAY NEWSOME. The History of
      a Southern State: North Carolina. Chapel Hill: Univer-
      sity of North Carolina Press, p. 597.
          Chesnutt mentioned as a prominent North Carolina writer
      of novels and short stories. Notes his receipt of the
      Spingarn Medal.

91

1954

4   LOGAN, RAYFORD W. <u>The Negro in American Life and Thought:</u>
     <u>The Nadir 1877-1901</u>. New York: The Dial Press, pp. 241,
     262, 333.
          Chesnutt's views on dialect writing are discussed and
     his books are considered. He was "the most eminent colored
     novelist" of his time, whose books were widely read because
     he was a skilled craftsman, not because he was black.

1955 A BOOKS - NONE

1955 B SHORTER WRITINGS

1   HUGHLEY, G. "Charles Waddell Chesnutt: Pioneer in the Fiction
     of Negro Life." <u>Negro History Bulletin</u>, 19 (December),
     54-55.
          A biographical and critical sketch for younger readers.
     Attempts to "show how Chesnutt helped to pave the way for
     the writing of the Negro Renaissance."

2   RICHARDS, ROBERT FULTON. <u>Concise Dictionary of American</u>
     <u>Literature</u>. New York: Philosophical Library, p. 28.
          A biographical and critical sketch, describing Chesnutt
     as "the first Negro writer to use the short story as a
     serious medium." "As a Negro writer, he was a pioneer in
     depicting the struggle of his race, during the post war
     years, in works regarded not only as important social
     treatises but also as artistic accomplishments."

3   WHITEMAN, MAXWELL. <u>A Century of Fiction by American Negroes</u>.
     Philadelphia: Maurice Jacobs, pp. 14-15.
          An annotated bibliography of Chesnutt's novels and
     books, of short stories.

1956 A BOOKS - NONE

1956 B SHORTER WRITINGS

1   BUTCHER, MARGARET JUST. <u>The Negro in American Culture</u>.
     New York: Alfred A. Knopf, pp. 162, 278.
          Chesnutt was "an early realist, the first Negro novelist
     to handle social themes artistically." Unlike Dunbar,
     Chesnutt sought to escape sentimental commonplaces and
     "counter the influence of the Thomas Nelson Page school of
     fiction and reveal a more balanced and accurate picture of
     Negro life in the South."

2   RICHARDSON, BEN. Great American Negroes. New York: Thomas Y.
        Crowell Co., p. 112. Chesnutt mentioned in a general con-
        sideration of black literature. The short story was his
        forte; his best works were The Conjure Woman and The House
        Behind the Cedars.

3   TURNER, ARLIN. George W. Cable: A Biography. Durham, North
        Carolina: Duke University Press, pp. 265, 269, 270.
        Chesnutt's activities in the Open Letter Club mentioned.

1957 A   BOOKS - NONE

1957 B   SHORTER WRITINGS

1   BRAITHWAITE, WILLIAM S. "Alain Locke's Relationship to the
        Negro in American Literature." Phylon, 18 (Second Quarter),
        166-73.
            Chesnutt and Dunbar are the two major figures in black
        writing at the turn of the century. "In Dunbar and Ches-
        nutt were first expressed the sensibility of an aesthetic
        form in Negro authorship that found evocation in the ade-
        quate techniques of specific artistic mediums."

2   BYRD, JAMES W. "Stereotypes of White Characters in Early
        Negro Novels." College Language Association Journal, 1
        (November), 28-35.
            Chesnutt discussed in a study of six major stereotypes
        of white men frequently found in novels written by blacks
        before World War I. His novels exhibit five major stereo-
        types: the benevolent white father of mulattos; the kind
        aristocrat; the poor-white villain; the brutal overseer;
        the northern champion of the negro.

1958 A   BOOKS - NONE

1958 B   SHORTER WRITINGS

1   BONE, ROBERT A. The Negro Novel in America. New Haven,
        Connecticut: Yale University Press, pp. 14, 18, 26, 29,
        35-38, 174.
            Chesnutt wrote novels of "the Talented Tenth." "An ap-
        praisal of Chesnutt's novels is hardly a fair measure of
        his talent. On the strength of his short stories alone, he
        raised the standards of Negro fiction to a new and higher
        plane. . . . In his novels, however, he became an overt
        propagandist, to the detriment of his art. Furthermore, he

1958

never succeeded in mastering the aesthetic requirements of the larger genre." Includes critical comment on three novels.

2   CADY, EDWIN H. The Realist at War: The Mature Years 1885-1920 of William Dean Howells. Syracuse, New York: Syracuse University Press, p. 208.
     Chesnutt mentioned briefly as a writer whose success was promoted by Howells.

3   MAGIL, FRANK N., ed. Cyclopedia of World Authors. New York: Harper and Row, p. 209.
     A biographical and critical sketch, with some primary and secondary bibliographical references. Chesnutt's two main interests were "the customs, folklore, and superstitions of Negroes, and the sociological and legal problems" that confronted blacks in America. The first interest produced art that was "quite similar to the Uncle Remus stories." The second, though commendable, was less artistically fruitful. It produced novels "in which the character and plot are often subordinated to propagandistic and didactic interests."

4   REDDING, J. SAUNDERS. The Lonesome Road: The Story of the Negro's Part in America. Garden City: Doubleday and Co., pp. 149-50.
     Chesnutt won literary distinction by writing uncompromisingly and impartially of blacks and whites. His works, however, particularly The Marrow of Tradition, The Colonel's Dream, and The House Behind the Cedars, tended to correct false views, and the white reading public paid little attention. Thus "a fine literary talent fizzed out like a drenched fire."

5   TURNER, ARLIN. "The Open Letter Club," in The Negro Question: A Selection of Writings on Civil Rights in the South, by George W. Cable. Edited by Arlin Turner. New York: Doubleday and Co., pp. 201, 205.
     Chesnutt mentioned as a scheduled participant with George W. Cable in a planned symposium on "The Economics of the Southern Question." Chesnutt and Cable were to argue in favor of greater education and fuller rights for blacks, but the sponsoring club was abandoned in the spring of 1890. Includes a letter from Cable to a "Mr. Boyd," dated December 30, 1889, defending Chesnutt's arguments on behalf of black rights.

1959 A BOOKS - NONE

1959 B SHORTER WRITINGS

1   ARDEN, EUGENE. "The Early Harlem Novel." Phylon, 20 (First
     Quarter), 25-31.
          Describes the beginnings of Harlem fiction, with analy-
     sis of Dunbar's The Sport of the Gods. In The Wife of His
     Youth, Chesnutt portrayed a "compulsive urge to imitate
     white values and the attacks of conscience which inevitably
     follow."

2   BARDOLPH, RICHARD. The Negro Vanguard. New York: Rinehart
     and Co., pp. 95-96, 155.
          A biographical and critical sketch. Chesnutt is "the
     most competent Negro writer of fiction before the 1920's."
     "Though it was on the color line that he found his ma-
     terials, he did not, in the manner of the later realists,
     use the novel for propaganda but for dramatizing human con-
     flicts, aspirations and anxieties." Despite the fact that
     "disillusionment ended his career as a professional lit-
     terateur," he was always a "race champion, scolding writers
     who traduced Negroes."

3   BUTCHER, PHILIP. George W. Cable: The Northampton Years.
     New York: Columbia University Press, pp. 23, 92-97, 122.
          Chesnutt's view of race relations at the turn of the
     century is noted, and his acquaintance with Cable is dis-
     cussed. Chesnutt was a member of the Open Letter Club, and
     Cable attempted to hire him as his secretary.

1960 A BOOKS - NONE

1960 B SHORTER WRITINGS

1   CLARKE, JOHN HENRIK. "Transition in the American Negro Short
     Story." Phylon, 21 (Fourth Quarter), 360-66.
          General survey of short stories by black American
     writers. Chesnutt was the first black writer "fully a
     master of the short story as a literary form." His novels
     "did not measure up to the standards" of his short stories.
     A "better writer" than Dunbar, "his style and attitude dif-
     fered radically." Chesnutt was "the most accomplished
     Negro writer" before Richard Wright.

2   SIMPSON, CLAUDE M., ed. The Local Colorists: American Short
     Stories, 1857-1900. New York: Harper and Brothers,
     pp. 191-192.

1960

> A biographical and critical sketch introducing a short
> story by Chesnutt. He was "one of the first American
> Negroes to write successful fiction." Chesnutt's two books
> of short stories are his best work. "The three novels that
> soon followed were substantial contributions to the so-
> ciology of race relations, but they were artistically
> weakened by his bitterness toward prevailing prejudices."

1961 A   BOOKS - NONE

1961 B   SHORTER WRITINGS

1   ANON. "Chesnutt Marker (Looking and Listening)." Crisis, 68
     (October), 494-95.
>   A biographical sketch and a notice that a monument has
> recently been erected to Chesnutt in Cumberland, North
> Carolina. Chesnutt was "not only the first distinguished
> Negro author of short stories and novels, but in some
> respects . . . among the foremost American novelists of
> his day."

1962 A   BOOKS

1   RENDER, SYLVIA LYONS. "Eagle With Clipped Wings: Form and
     Feeling in the Fiction of Charles Waddell Chesnutt." Ph.D.
     dissertation, George Peabody College for Teachers.
>   "This dissertation attempts an analytical and inter-
> pretive study of Chesnutt's published imaginative prose
> works to determine the extent and significance of his con-
> tribution to American literature. . . . Each selection is
> considered within the context of the period it reflects as
> well as in the framework of Chesnutt's related non-imagina-
> tive writings, popular and critical opinion, the author's
> private papers and statements of relatives and friends.
> . . . Special attention is paid to the portrayal of Negro
> character and to interracial relations."

1962 B   SHORTER WRITINGS

1   BONTEMPS, ARNA. One Hundred Years of Negro Freedom.
     New York: Dodd, Mead and Co., pp. 183-86, 209, 211, 229,
     262.
>   Chesnutt's relationship with Booker T. Washington is
> discussed and his views on Washington's solution to the
> race problem are considered. Although Chesnutt was a friend

of Washington, he had considerable reservations and doubts about Washington's platform, and he continually withheld his endorsement. Quotes from a letter written by Chesnutt to Washington, outlining his position on race matters.

2 BUTCHER, PHILIP. George W. Cable. New York: Twayne Publishers, pp. 98, 106, 119, 163.
    Mentions that Chesnutt was a member of the Open Letter Club, and that Cable gave advice regarding The House Behind the Cedars.

3 CHESNUTT, HELEN M. "Charles Waddell Chesnutt," in Ohio Authors and Their Books. Edited by William Coyle. Cleveland: World Publishing Co., pp. 113-115.
    A biographical sketch treating Chesnutt's life and activities, but focusing on his literary achievements. Each book by Chesnutt is critically evaluated, and its public and financial success is noted.

4 HERZBERG, MAX J., ed. The Readers' Encyclopedia of American Literature. New York: Thomas Y. Crowell Co., p. 170.
    A biographical and critical sketch. Chesnutt is the first black novelist. His early work resembles that of Joel Chandler Harris, and his later work focuses on racial prejudice. He was "a pioneer author."

5 McMAHAN, MARGARET. "A Tar Heel Literary Pioneer." Fayetteville (North Carolina) Observer (11 November).
    A biographical sketch lauding Chesnutt as a writer and noting his connection to Fayetteville. "He was one of the first North Carolinians of either race to make a national name for himself in the field of letters."

6 SMITH, ROBERT A. "A Note on the Folktales of Charles Waddell Chesnutt." College Language Association Journal, 5 (March), 229-32.
    A consideration of The Conjure Woman. Each story is mentioned, and the function and purpose of Uncle Julius is discussed. "A fair estimate of The Conjure Woman will show that it is a good attempt as a 'first,' and as such, seems not to suffer when compared to other collections of the same nature."

1963

1963 A BOOKS - NONE

1963 B SHORTER WRITINGS

1   ADAMS, RUSSELL L. Great Negroes Past and Present. Chicago:
       Afro-American Publishing Co., pp. 147, 151.
            Chesnutt was the first black writer to give serious con-
       sideration to the artistic requirements of the novel and
       short story. He was also the first black writer to rise
       above the "double standard" of literary criticism and be
       judged directly as an American writer. A biographical
       sketch is included.

2   CHAPMAN, ABRAHAM, ed. Black Voices: An Anthology of Afro-
       American Literature. New York: St. Martin's Press,
       pp. 50-51.
            A biographical sketch introducing a selection of Ches-
       nutt's work. Chesnutt was "the first Negro writer in the
       United States to master the short story form and the craft
       of fiction." Howells' article, "Mr. Charles W. Chesnutt's
       Stories," is quoted to show the reaction occasioned by
       Chesnutt's work. See 1900.B104.

3   JONES, LeROI. Blues People. New York: Morrow House,
       pp. 58-59, 132.
            An incident in Chesnutt's novel The Marrow of Tradition
       is discussed to show how the idea of white superiority was
       accepted by many members of "the better class of Negroes."
       This is an aspect of the slave mentality.

4   MEIER, AUGUST. Negro Thought in America, 1880-1915. Ann
       Arbor: University of Michigan Press, pp. 110, 155-56,
       243-44, 264, 266, 268-69, 275, 277.
            Chesnutt was a writer and attorney who "adopted a con-
       sistently uncompromising philosophy of assimilation and
       protest." His views of social and racial problems are con-
       sidered, and his relationship with Booker T. Washington is
       explored.

5   SPILLER, ROBERT E., et al. Literary History of the United
       States: History. Third edition, revised. New York: The
       Macmillan Co., pp. 854-55.
            Chesnutt and Dunbar are "noteworthy followers in the
       wake of [Joel Chandler] Harris." Chesnutt's short stories
       are considered briefly. Both Chesnutt and Dunbar "brought
       to their work the stamp of their pervasive personalities,
       and both enriched that branch of nineteenth century litera-
       ture which relates to the old-time Southern Negro."

1964 A BOOKS - NONE

1964 B SHORTER WRITINGS

1   JARRETT, CALVIN D. "A Negro Novelist Remembered." Negro
    Digest, 13 (October), 38-45.
        A biographical sketch, with some critical evaluation.
    Chesnutt is "one of the first North Carolinians of either
    race to make a national name for himself in the field of
    letters." His books are mentioned briefly. The House Be-
    hind the Cedars is in the first rank of Chesnutt's novels
    and The Marrow of Tradition is an American classic.

2   KAISER, ERNEST. "Literature on the South." Freedomways, 4
    (Winter), 149-67.
        Chesnutt's writing, and that of other southern blacks,
    is more powerful and faithful to black life than is the
    writing of southern white writers.

3   QUARLES, BENJAMIN. The Negro in the Making of America.
    London: Collier-Macmillan, Ltd., p. 201.
        Chesnutt was a "most able" early black novelist whose
    novels "realistically depicted the lot of the mulatto."

4   REDDING, J. SAUNDERS. "The Problems of the Negro Writer."
    Massachusetts Review, 6 (Autumn-Winter), 57-70.
        In a consideration of the "literary ghetto" where black
    American writers are often placed, it is common that "the
    standard anthologies do not contain the works of Charles W.
    Chesnutt, who was a far better novelist than his much
    better known contemporary William Dean Howells."

1965 A BOOKS - NONE

1965 B SHORTER WRITINGS

1   BERTHOFF, WARNER. The Ferment of Realism: American Literature
    1884-1919. New York: The Free Press, p. xiv.
        Offers a list of books in the preface that are "readable
    and accomplished works we should be the poorer for losing
    sight of," even though "I have not managed to find a place"
    for discussing them. Chesnutt's The Conjure Woman is one
    of these.

2   HART, JAMES D. The Oxford Companion to American Literature.
    Fourth edition. New York: Oxford University Press, p. 150.

1965

A brief critical sketch. Chesnutt is best known for his short stories, particularly The Conjure Woman. His novels are less successful.

3   JAHN, JANHEINZ. A Bibliography of Neo-African Literature from Africa, America, and the Caribbean. New York: Frederick A. Praeger, pp. 233-34.
Chesnutt is noted as a North American writer and his published books are listed.

4   RENDER, SYLVIA LYONS. "Tar Heelia in Chesnutt." College Language Association Journal, 9 (September), 39-50.
A study of Chesnutt's use of North Carolina folklore in his work, especially in The Conjure Woman. "Charles W. Chesnutt's unique depiction of North Carolina scene guarantees him a permanent place in American literary history." Though Chesnutt eventually "left the Tar Heel State in fact, he remained in spirit. He could not get North Carolina off his mind."

5   WINKELMAN, DONALD M. "Three American Authors as Semi-Folk Artists." Journal of American Folklore, 78 (April-June), 130-35.
Considers Mark Twain, Mary Wade Wellman, and Chesnutt as writers who are not folk artists, but do incorporate folklore into their works. This illuminates folklore's effect on the creative process. Chesnutt's use of folklore is "artificial--the borrowing of material from a foreign group." "The Negro folklore of Charles Waddell Chestnutt's [sic] books is interesting, but Chestnutt [sic] is the bemused gentleman who, after the tale, says, 'That is a very ingenious fairy tale . . . and we are much obliged to you.'"

1966 A   BOOKS - NONE

1966 B   SHORTER WRITINGS

1   BONTEMPS, ARNA. "The Negro Contribution to American Letters," in The American Negro Reference Book. Edited by John P. Davis. Englewood Cliffs, New Jersey: Prentice Hall, pp. 851-78.
Chesnutt was a turn of the century writer who "attained an objectivity of vision in keeping with his technical skills, while at the same time facing up to the sociological realities." Chesnutt's books are briefly considered.

Charles W. Chesnutt: A Reference Guide

2   CHAPMAN, ABRAHAM. The Negro in American Literature and a
    Bibliography of Literature By and About Negroes. Oshkosh,
    Wisconsin: Wisconsin Council of Teachers of English, p. 44.
       Chesnutt's books of short stories and his novels are
    listed in a section devoted to fiction.

3   CLARKE, JOHN HENRIK. "Introduction," in American Negro Short
    Stories. Edited by John Henrik Clarke. New York: Hill
    and Wang, pp. xv-xvi.
       Chesnutt is "the Negro master of the short story form."
    Like Paul Laurence Dunbar, he reached a larger general read-
    ing audience than any black writer who had come before. His
    best stories drew on his memories of the traditions and
    superstitions of blacks in his home state of North Carolina.

4   GONZÁLEZ, JOSÉ LUIZ. "Los Primeros Novelistas Negros Norte
    Americanos." Casa de las Americas, 6 (36/37), 98-114.
       Chesnutt, Dunbar, and James Weldon Johnson are important
    turn of the century authors. DuBois' term "talented tenth"
    is used to describe their backgrounds and to explain their
    efforts to improve the status of their race. Their works
    are related to these efforts.

5   GROSS, SEYMOUR L. "Introduction: Stereotype to Archetype:
    The Negro in American Literary Criticism," in Images of the
    Negro in American Literature. Edited by Seymour L. Gross
    and John E. Hardy. Chicago: University of Chicago Press,
    pp. 8, 9, 17.
       Chesnutt and other black writers gave the black American
    "a sense of cultural worth and achievement that would no
    longer allow him to sit complacently still for his tradi-
    tional portraits."

6   HILL, HERBERT, ed. Anger and Beyond: The Negro Writer in the
    United States. New York: Harper and Row, pp. 3-4, 6, 36,
    54.
       Chesnutt is "the best writer of prose fiction that the
    race has produced." The record of his publication is con-
    sidered. When his first book was published, his race was
    not mentioned in order to promote sales. His later books,
    published after his race was known, failed to sell well for
    another reason. They dealt honestly with the problems of
    race and often contradicted accepted stereotypes of the day.

7   JONES, LeROI. Home: Social Essays. New York: William
    Morrow and Co., pp. 105-107.
       Chesnutt is mentioned in a discussion of the general
    mediocrity of black literature. Black literature has not

1966

been comparable to black music because it has been dominated largely be middle class writers like Chesnutt, whose
"embarassing and inverted paternalism" and "refined 'Afro-
American' heroes are far cries from the richness and pro-
fundity of the blues."

8   LITTLEJOHN, DAVID. Black on White: A Critical Survey of
Writings by American Negroes. New York: Grossman Publishers, pp. 27-29, 46.
A brief critical study. Like Dunbar, Chesnutt wrote in
the plantation tradition, but unlike him, Chesnutt shows
more clearly the truths of its decay. "Chesnutt's novels
and stories are distinctly professional, minor works of the
American Gilded Age, with all the limitations of diction,
technique, and moral horizon that that implies. But he is
never mean or stupid, and affords at his best some agree-
able hours reading to those who can make allowances for
sixty years."

9   MASUOKA, JITSUICHI. The American Race Problem. New York:
Thomas Y. Crowell Co., p. 286. A general consideration of
black American literature is included. "Prior to the recent decades, the only fiction worthy of mention written by
Negroes is perhaps that of Charles W. Chesnutt." Chesnutt's
stories had considerable vogue.

10 MEIER, AUGUST and ELLIOTT M. RUDWICK. From Plantation to
Ghetto: An Interpretive History of American Negroes.
New York: Hill and Wang, p. 208.
Chesnutt was a literary artist at the turn of the century
who explored folk culture in a serious way, unlike Paul
Laurence Dunbar. His novels were "vigorous protests against
American racism."

11 NICHOLSON, JOHN B., JR. "Introduction," in Baxter's
Procrustes. Cleveland: Rowfant Club.
A biographical essay in a limited edition of "Baxter's
Procrustes." One-hundred-eighty copies were printed. The
story appeared in Atlantic, June, 1904. Chesnutt had been
a member of this club of book collecters during his lifetime.

12 WOODWARD, C. VANN. The Strange Career of Jim Crow. New York:
Oxford University Press, p. 96.
An account of Chesnutt's views on black rights in 1903.
At this time "the rights of the Negroes are at a lower ebb
than at any time during the thirty-five years of their
freedom, and the race prejudice is more intense and more
uncompromising."

13   WRIGHT, LYLE H. <u>American Fiction 1876-1900: A Contribution
      Toward a Bibliography</u>. San Marino, California: The
      Huntington Library, pp. 101-102.
            Annotates two books of short stories by Chesnutt, and
      <u>The House Behind the Cedars</u>.

<u>1967 A BOOKS - NONE</u>

<u>1967 B SHORTER WRITINGS</u>

1   KATZ, WILLIAM LOREN. <u>Eyewitness: The Negro in American
      History</u>. New York: Pitman Publishing Corporation, p. 321.
            <u>The Marrow of Tradition</u> is mentioned in conjunction with
      the Wilmington, North Carolina, riot of 1898.

2   MASON, JULIAN D., JR. "Charles W. Chesnutt as Southern
      Author." <u>Mississippi Quarterly</u>, 20 (Spring), 77-89.
            The usual failure to treat Chesnutt's "Southerness" is
      a disservice to him, to his fiction, to the south, and to
      the "integrity and accuracy of histories of Southern litera-
      ture." The south nourished Chesnutt's ambition, concerns,
      spirit, conscience, manners, understanding of life, and
      his writing. Chesnutt had a "very real love and respect
      for the South and its best aspects." Primarily a biography,
      brief analyses of Chesnutt's major works are included.

3   PLOSKI, HARRY A. and ROSCOE E. BROWN. <u>The Negro Almanac</u>.
      New York: Bellwether Publishing Co., pp. 169, 682.
            A biographical sketch focusing on Chesnutt's literary
      work. He was the first black writer of the "problem
      novel." Much of his art was "basically ingratiating," and
      was later rejected by the writers of the "Harlem School."

4   RENDER, SYLVIA LYONS. "North Carolina Dialect: Chesnutt
      Style." <u>North Carolina Folklore</u>, 15 (November), 67-70.
            Studies Chesnutt's use of North Carolina dialect and
      folk speech in his fiction. In using dialect, Chesnutt was
      able to maintain the rhythms and intonations of the speak-
      ing voice, as well as to make the fine distinctions between
      the language of different races and classes. He provided
      additional local color by using particular regional words
      and homely sayings. "By artistically reproducing folk
      speech in his fiction, Chesnutt lent greater verisimilitude
      to his works and removed the barrier of time or space, or
      both, between many readers and a North Carolina of the
      past."

1967

5   ROBINSON, WILHELMENA S. Historical Negro Biographies.
     New York: Publishers Co., p. 174.
          A biographical sketch.

6   TURNER, DARWIN T. "The Negro Novelist and the South."
     Southern Humanities Review, 1 (Spring), 21-29.
          A general survey of black writing on the south. Ches-
     nutt "wrote excellent short stories which draw upon the
     folklore and the attitudes of Negroes more perceptively
     than do the more famous tales of Joel Chandler Harris."

1968 A BOOKS

1   FOSTER, CHARLES W. "The Representation of Negro Dialect in
     Charles W. Chesnutt's The Conjure Woman." Ph.D. disserta-
     tion, University of Alabama.
          An analysis of the dialect of North Carolina blacks as
     it appears in these stories. The study utilizes field
     records for the Linguistic Atlas of the South Atlantic
     States, stored at the University of Chicago. Chesnutt was
     remarkably accurate in his representation of the dialect
     for the area around Fayetteville. "He does not exploit
     dialect for its own sake, but depends on its accurate use
     for additional depth of character development in Uncle
     Julius."

1968 B SHORTER WRITINGS

1   BROWN, STERLING. The Negro in American Fiction. Port Wash-
     ington, New York: Kennikat Press, pp. 78-82.
          Reprint of 1937.B3.

2   BUTCHER, PHILIP. "George W. Cable and George W. Williams:
     An Abortive Collaboration." Journal of Negro History, 53
     (October), 334-44.
          Chesnutt was "the only Negro member" of the Open Letter
     Club, founded by Cable to promote "constructive discussion
     of the problem of the New South" and to publish "carefully
     prepared statements likely to promote the interests of
     Negroes and poor whites."

3   CLARKE, JOHN HENRIK. "The Origin and Growth of Afro-American
     Literature." Journal of Human Relations, 16 (Third
     Quarter), 368-84.
          In a survey of black writers from the middle eighteenth
     century to the present, Chesnutt is mentioned with Dunbar

as two of the important writers during the Progressive Era
and the Gilded Age.

4   DROTNING, PHILLIP P. A Guide to Negro History in America.
    New York: Doubleday and Co., p. 145.
        Chesnutt mentioned as important in the black history of
    North Carolina and Fayetteville State Teacher's College,
    where he was principal at one time.

5   EMANUEL, JAMES A. and THEODORE L. GROSS, eds. Dark Symphony:
    Negro Literature in America. New York: The Free Press,
    pp. 2-3, 4, 7, 9, 25-26, 64, 199, 352, 353.
        Chesnutt mentioned primarily in a biographical and
    critical sketch introducing one of his short stories. "Al-
    though Chesnutt's three novels break some new ground in
    their picture of Negroes during Reconstruction years--for
    example, the exploration of 'passing' in the first novel--
    the author's achievement as a short story writer upholds
    his reputation."

6   F. C. S. "Charles Waddell Chesnutt," in The Conjure Woman.
    1899. Reprint. Ridgewood, New Jersey: Gregg Press.
        A biographical and critical sketch. Chesnutt was "the
    first important Negro writer." Considers the critical re-
    ception of The Conjure Woman, compares it to the stories
    of Joel Chandler Harris, and comments on its "rich and
    varied" language.

7   _____. "Charles Waddell Chesnutt," in The House Behind the
    Cedars. 1900. Reprint. Ridgewood, New Jersey: Gregg
    Press.
        A biographical sketch. Chesnutt was "the first American
    Negro novelist." Brief critical commentary on Chesnutt's
    books included. The House Behind the Cedars was "the first
    American novel to deal with the moral and social problems
    faced by Negroes who can 'pass' for white."

8   GARTNER, CAROL B. "Charles W. Chesnutt: Novelist of a
    Cause." Markham Review, 1 (October), 5-12.
        Surveys the recent criticism of Chesnutt. Gives a
    biographical sketch. Considers Chesnutt's views on the
    "race question," and deals with each of his books. The
    Conjure Woman is his best book, and the novels are not at
    all as strong. "He seems to have vacillated within himself
    between writing for the purpose of exploring race problems
    and advancing the colored people and writing to create fine
    literature."

1968

9   HASLAM, GERALD W.   "'The Sheriff's Children': Chesnutt's
     Tragic Racial Parable." Negro American Literature Forum, 2
     (Summer), 21-25.
         The story "succinctly summarizes the moral dilemma in-
     herent in chattel slavery" and is an "apt parable" for
     America's continuing racial crisis. It represents a high
     point in nineteenth century American black literature. "By
     emphasizing the white father rather than the mulatto son,"
     Chesnutt "partially avoided the melodramatic stereotypes
     which marred so much of his work."

10   JAHN, JANHEINZ. Neo-African Literature: A History of Black
     Writing. New York: Grove Press, pp. 131, 141, 150-51,
     154, 204.
         Chesnutt is compared to Paul Laurence Dunbar. Chesnutt
     was "a disciple of the naturalist school, and in The Wife
     of His Youth, for instance, placed the central figure of
     each story in an abnormal situation caused by racial
     prejudice." This method looked forward to Richard Wright
     and the twentieth century.

11   KELLER, DEAN H. "Charles Waddell Chesnutt (1858-1932)."
     American Literary Realism, 1870-1910, 3 (Summer), 1-4.
         A bibliographical essay surveying the present state and
     the history of criticism of Chesnutt. Surveys editions of
     Chesnutt's works, reprints, manuscripts, and collections,
     and indicates new research areas.

12   MARGOLIES, EDWARD. Native Sons: A Critical Study of
     Twentieth Century Black American Authors. Philadelphia:
     J. B. Lippincott Co., pp. 24-25, 30.
         Brief biographical sketch and critical comment that
     deals primarily with The Conjure Woman. "Perhaps Ches-
     nutt's chief distinction is not, as has sometimes been
     pointed out, that he was the first Negro to employ the
     short story form with a modicum of popular success, . . .
     but that he was the first Negro to tap the rich vein of
     Negro folk culture."

13   MIERS, EARLE SCHENCK. "Introduction," in The Wife of His
     Youth. 1899. Reprint. Ann Arbor: University of Michigan
     Press, pp. v-xiv.
         A biographical and critical sketch placing Chesnutt in
     the context of his times. Chesnutt was "the first American
     Negro literary figure of enduring distinction." His first
     two books are his best, and in his shorter sketches, he
     "may well rank with such American masters of the craft as
     Mark Twain and Bret Harte."

14   WESLEY, CHARLES H. The Quest for Equality: From Civil War to
      Civil Rights. New York: Publishers Co., p. 158.
         Chesnutt is one of only two black authors who wrote
      before the twenties who was of "consequence."

1969 A BOOKS - NONE

1969 B SHORTER WRITINGS

1   BERGMAN, PETER M. The Chronicle History of the Negro in
     America. New York: Harper and Row, pp. 299, 326, 332,
     335, 346.
        Comments on each of Chesnutt's published books. His
     works are among the first works of prose fiction written by
     an American black to reach a mass white audience.

2   DAVIS, RUSSELL H. Memorable Negroes in Cleveland's Past.
     Cleveland: Western Reserve Historical Society, pp. 28-30.
        A biographical sketch and brief critical comment.
     Chesnutt was "a master in the difficult art of short story
     writing" and "the first Negro novelist and short story
     writer in the United States." Comments on Chesnutt's
     papers at Fisk University. See 1954.A1; 1973.A1.

3   FARNSWORTH, ROBERT M. "Introduction," in The Conjure Woman.
     1899. Reprint. Ann Arbor: University of Michigan Press,
     pp. v-xix.
        Chesnutt's book is in the "plantation story" tradition.
     It "abandons the sentimental fantasy of plantation life"
     by being "deliberately contrived to condition or enlighten
     a white audience without forcing a direct emotional con-
     frontation." Summarizes several stories to show that Ches-
     nutt "evokes a strong sense of discreteness between the
     black world and the white." "By the end of the book Uncle
     Julius emerges as a shrewd and wise old man." See 1973.B13.

4   _____. "Introduction," in The Marrow of Tradition. 1901.
     Reprint. Ann Arbor: University of Michigan Press,
     pp. v-xvii.
        A biographical and critical sketch. "Chesnutt's fiction
     is a history of varyingly successful attempts to picture
     the world of the nineteenth century Negro as it really was
     in terms palatable to an almost exclusively white American
     book-buying public." The Marrow of Tradition was Chesnutt's
     last such effort. "With all its obtrusive plotting and
     frequently melodramatic sentiment, it was the most compre-
     hensively realistic picture of the black man's dilemma in
     the South yet to be published in American fiction."

1969

5   FARNSWORTH, ROBERT M. "Testing the Color Line--Dunbar and
    Chesnutt," in The Black American Writer: Fiction. Edited
    by C. W. E. Bigsby. Deland, Florida: Everett/Edwards,
    pp. 111-124.
        A comparison of the writing of Chesnutt and Paul Laurence
    Dunbar, the first black writers to achieve prominence during
    the post-Reconstruction period. "In a sense Charles Ches-
    nutt was to Paul Laurence Dunbar what W. E. B. DuBois was
    to Booker T. Washington." Although Dunbar knew how to ex-
    ploit his audience, his work does not "look forward."
    Chesnutt was more alive to the currents of literary and
    social change. He disciplined himself better than Dunbar
    to careful, realistic documentation. "Dunbar seemed wist-
    fully to believe in the near possibility of a truly color-
    less world. Chesnutt was more pragmatic, believing perhaps
    in the same ultimate vision, but realizing more prominently
    the immediate problems of Southern disfranchisement, Jim
    Crow legislation, and racial intermarriage."

6   MASON, JULIAN D., JR. "Charles W. Chesnutt (1858-1932)," in
    A Bibliographical Guide to the Study of Southern Litera-
    ture. Edited by Louis D. Rubin, Jr. Baton Rouge:
    Louisiana State University Press, pp. 171-73.
        A bibliographic essay and list of secondary sources.
    Helen Chesnutt's biography is indispensable. The best cur-
    rent scholarly work is being done by Sylvia Render. See
    1952.A1; 1962.A1; 1965.B4; 1967.B4; 1969.B7; 1974.B6.

7   RENDER, SYLVIA LYONS. "Introduction," in The Marrow of
    Tradition. 1901. Reprint. New York: Arno Press,
    pp. i-vii.
        A biographical and critical sketch. Views Chesnutt's
    life in the light of both his artistic work and his concern
    with the problems of race. The Marrow of Tradition is "a
    landmark in American literature." A social novel, based on
    the Wilmington, North Carolina, riot of 1898, it follows
    both black and national literary tradition. Although none
    of the situations in the novel are altogether new, it in-
    troduces new character types to American fiction.

8   RUBIN, LOUIS D., JR. George W. Cable: The Life and Times of
    a Southern Heretic. New York: Pegasus, p. 201.
        Chesnutt is mentioned with regard to his membership in
    the Open Letter Club.

9   SOCKEN, JUNE. "Charles Waddell Chesnutt and the Solution to
    the Race Problem." Negro American Literature Forum, 3
    (Summer), 52-56.

An examination of "some of the perceptive, and still relevant, ideas put forth by Charles Chesnutt." Considers the fictional themes of miscegenation, the black's acceptance of white cultural values, and the identity crisis of the mulatto. The issue of assimilation, which Chesnutt spoke of frequently in his non-fiction writing, is his solution to the race problem.

10   THORNBROUGH, EMMA LOU. <u>Great Lives Observed: Booker T. Washington</u>. Englewood Cliffs, New Jersey: Prentice-Hall, pp. 3, 20.
        Gives Chesnutt's views on Washington's political and educational philosophy. Although Chesnutt was "mildly critical and satirical" concerning Washington's overemphasis on industrial education, he paid tribute to Washington's "eminent services," and he approved of Washington's attempts to gain the support of the white south.

11   TURNER, DARWIN T. "Introduction," in <u>The House Behind the Cedars</u>. 1900. Reprint. Riverside, New Jersey: Collier Books, pp. vii-xx.
        A biographical and critical sketch. Chesnutt's stories are considered, particularly "The Goophered Grapevine" and "The Sheriff's Children." Chesnutt refused to use contemporary black stereotypes. His novels are "artistically inferior to his stories," often showing sentimentalizing, idealization, and melodramatic coincidence, and, polemic tendencies. <u>The House Behind the Cedars</u> is probably "the first story in which an author explored the problems of Americans who conceal their African heritage."

1970 A BOOKS

1   BELL, BERNARD W. "The Afroamerican Novel and Its Tradition." Ph.D. dissertation, University of Massachusetts.
        A study of seven black American novels, including <u>The Marrow of Tradition</u>. Considers ways in which black novelists respond similarly to white novelists, and ways in which they are unique. "Black novelists have generally acknowledged a dual responsibility: to their people and to their craft." Thus the black novel has been used to counteract stereotypes and to affirm the values of black life, but it has also acknowledged the importance of craftsmanship.

2   HEERMANCE, J. NOEL. "Charles W. Chesnutt: The Artist, the Man, and His Times." Ph.D. dissertation, Howard University.

1970

Considers Chesnutt's social environment, his personal attitudes and interests, and his writings. "This paper makes two major contributions to our understanding of Chesnutt. . . . It offers an honest and realistic understanding of him as a man," and it treats him as a "gifted and sophisticated artist."

1970 B   SHORTER WRITINGS

1   CORRIGAN, ROBERT A. "Bibliography of Afro-American Fiction 1853-1970." Studies in Black Literature, 1 (Summer), 57.
   A listing of six books by Chesnutt, and a general introduction treating problems of bibliography in Afro-American literature.

2   DANIEL, NEIL. "Chesnutt, Wright, and Jones: Some Uses of Stereotypes." Proceedings of Conference of College Teachers of English of Texas, 35 (September), 16-21.
   Chesnutt is related to "the role of black writers in American literature and the pattern of clichés which dominated the portrayal of black characters." Chesnutt had two goals as a writer of short stories: to establish himself as a successful and critically respected writer, and to break the stereotypes of blacks in popular American fiction. He did not reach his first goal, and although he successfully challenged popular black stereotypes, he did not destroy them.

3   FARNSWORTH, ROBERT M. "Charles Chesnutt and the Color Line," in Minor American Novelists. Edited by Charles A. Hoyt. Carbondale, Illinois: Southern Illinois University Press, pp. 28-40.
   Offers a "contemporary review" of Chesnutt's achievement and career. The Conjure Woman presents "the steadily sardonic view of slavery that one might expect from a Negro writer as opposed to the more romantically tinged . . . views of his white contemporaries, but these stories ruffled no feathers." The Wife of His Youth was more daring. Chesnutt's three novels are considered primarily in terms of his hopes for them, and their sales. The Colonel's Dream is "an all white novel" that did not disturb the tranquillity of Chesnutt's quiet success.

4   FARRISON, W. EDWARD. "What American Negro Literature Exists and Who Should Teach It?" College Language Association Journal, 13 (June), 374-81.

Surveys very early black American writers, emphasizing bibliographies and sources for effective teaching of the literature. Chesnutt mentioned as a black writer often described as early, when in fact he is not. Current research indicates that Afro-American literature began with Lucy Terry, about 1746.

5 FONER, ERIC. America's Black Past: A Reader in Afro-American History. New York: Harper and Row, pp. 274, 379.
Chesnutt was a prominent turn of the century writer who disagreed with Booker T. Washington about black advancement.

6 GANT, LISBETH A. "Charles Chesnutt--Forgotten Mastermind." Freedomways, 10 (Fourth Quarter), 326-32.
Chesnutt pioneered in exploring themes of contemporary pertinence to black people. Considers two short stories from The Wife of His Youth.

7 HASLAM, GERALD W., ed. Forgotten Pages of American Literature. Boston: Houghton Mifflin Co., pp. 10, 246, 255.
An anthology of ethnic American literature. Includes a brief biographical and critical sketch of Chesnutt. He was "one of the most important transitional figures in Afro-American literature," and paved the way for writing of the twenties.

8 HEMENWAY, ROBERT, ed. Introduction to "Social Realism in Charles W. Chesnutt," by Russell Ames. The Black Novelist. Columbus, Ohio: Charles E. Merrill, pp. 23-24.
Chesnutt was a "protege of William Dean Howells," and "dealt with a more realistic subject matter than previous black novelists." However, "his novels appear frequently over-written and are often disappointing." See 1953.B1.

9 KEARNS, FRANCIS E., ed. The Black Experience: An Anthology of American Literature for the 1970's. New York: The Viking Press, pp. 281-82.
A biographical and critical sketch introducing a short story. Chesnutt was the "first Negro short-story writer to attract a national audience." Like Paul Laurence Dunbar, he is at times accused of presenting an accommodationist point of view, particularly in his novels. Unlike Dunbar, however, he often gives the plantation tradition an ironic twist that conveys a bitter indictment of slavery.

10 LEARY, LEWIS. Articles on American Literature 1950-1967. Durham, North Carolina: Duke University Press, p. 54.
A list of eight articles dealing with Chesnutt.

1970

11   LOGAN, RAYFORD W., and IRVING S. COHEN. The American Negro:
      Old World Background and New World Experience. Boston:
      Houghton Mifflin Co., p. 144.
          Chesnutt was one of the most outstanding black writers
      at the end of the nineteenth century. He was the most
      popular black novelist in America.

12   OVINGTON, MARY W. The Walls Came Tumbling Down. New York:
      Shocken Books, pp. 19, 214, 238.
          Chesnutt was a writer concerned with the foibles of
      mulattos. Mentions his receiving the Spingarn Medal.

13   TURNER, DARWIN T. Afro-American Writers. New York:
      Appleton-Century-Crofts, pp. 44-45, 111.
          A bibliography of Chesnutt's books, and a selected
      secondary bibliography citing bibliography, biography, and
      criticism.

14   _____. Black American Literature: Essays, Poetry, Fiction,
      Drama. Columbus, Ohio: Charles E. Merrill Publishing
      Co., p. 297.
          Introduction to a short story. Chesnutt was "the first
      Afro-American to master the short story as an art form."
      Contains a brief biographical and critical sketch. Ches-
      nutt's most significant contribution to American literature
      may be the tales of The Conjure Woman.

15   WALSER, RICHARD. Literary North Carolina: A Brief Historical
      Survey. Raleigh, North Carolina: State Department of
      Archives and History, pp. 29, 30-31, 33, 59-60, 63.
          Chesnutt was among a group of writers who, in their
      "highly dramatic fiction, drew upon the war and its after-
      math to depict the turbulent social changes under way in
      North Carolina." As a black spokesman, Chesnutt "had the
      distinction of being the first Negro American writer to
      receive serious attention as a literary artist." The
      Conjure Woman is his best book.

16   WILLIAMS, KENNY J. They Also Spoke: An Essay on Negro
      Literature in America, 1787-1930. Nashville, Tennessee:
      Townsend Press, pp. 218-19, 223, 224, 225, 238, 248, 262,
      270, 276.
          Chesnutt's fiction was in the traditions of plantation
      fiction, "raceless" fiction, and social protest fiction.
      The Conjure Woman "shows the plantation tradition at its
      finest point." Chesnutt did not write many "raceless"
      stories. "Racial prejudice in all its ramifications forms
      the central theme of much of what Chesnutt wrote."

Charles W. Chesnutt: A Reference Guide

1971 A BOOKS - NONE

1971 B SHORTER WRITINGS

1   BAKER, HOUSTON A., JR. Black Literature in America. New York:
     McGraw-Hill Book Co., pp. 4-7.
         An anthology of black American literature. Chesnutt is
     mentioned in the introduction, and in a section devoted to
     early fiction, poetry, and criticism. He was a "conscious
     literary artist who made use of the folk experiences of
     the black American." He was "the first black American fic-
     tion writer of distinction. . . . Chesnutt's novels tend
     to be overly polemical, but in his short stories he handles
     language, symbol, and wit with consumate skill." Some of
     his best stories are "The Goophered Grapevine," "The Bou-
     quet," and "A Matter of Principle."

2   BALDWIN, RICHARD E. "The Art of The Conjure Woman," American
     Literature, 43 (November), 385-98.
         In these stories, Chesnutt "avoids stifling sterotypes
     while criticizing the myths of white supremacy and demon-
     strating the range and quality of black experience" to a
     degree never achieved in his "realistic fiction." Ches-
     nutt's central problem was his audience. His conjure
     stories achieve "a near-tragic, near-comic lyricism." His
     technique relies heavily on irony.

3   CHAMETZKY, JULES. "Regional Literature and Ethnic Realities."
     Antioch Review, 31 (Fall), 385-96.
         Primarily a consideration of Chesnutt's short stories.
     In these, Chesnutt created the "first conscious, fictional
     form given to the black ethos in America." Consequently,
     whites seldom understood the import of Chesnutt's ironic
     tales, which bespeak so well the black experience. John,
     the white northerner in The Conjure Woman, is a good ex-
     ample of this. Only after Chesnutt despaired of his audi-
     ence examining his work closely enough to get below its
     surface did he change his attack to a more obvious front.
     This resulted in the more direct message of his novels.

4   DANCE, DARYL CUMBER. "Wit and Humor in Black American
     Literature." Ph.D. dissertation, University of Virginia.
         Considers humor in black American literature beginning
     with black American folklore and ending with the works of
     modern writers. Chesnutt is included in a survey of writers
     who show that "the black man has found laughter a means of
     maintaining his sanity and of making life possible in a
     mad, cruel world--a means of survival."

1971

5   DAVIS, ARTHUR P., and J. SAUNDERS REDDING, eds. <u>Cavalcade:</u>
<u>Negro American Writing from 1760 to the Present</u>. New York:
Houghton Mifflin Co., pp. 168-69.
    A biographical sketch introducing a short story. Ches-
nutt was "undoubtedly the best black fiction writer before
Richard Wright."

6   FORD, NICK AARON. <u>Black Insights: Significant Literature by</u>
<u>Black Americans--1760 to the Present</u>. Waltham, Massachu-
setts: Ginn and Co., pp. xvi, xvii, 50, 57, 219.
    Chesnutt was one of the first black Americans to win a
reputation for short stories. A biographical sketch and a
quotation from Hugh Gloster's <u>Negro Voices in American</u>
<u>Fiction</u> regarding Chesnutt's literary achievements are
given as an introduction to "The Wife of His Youth."
<u>See</u> 1948.B4.

7   GROSS, THEODORE L. <u>The Heroic Ideal in American Literature</u>.
New York: The Free Press, pp. 130, 132, 135.
    Chesnutt's work is considered with that of Paul Laurence
Dunbar as an "imaginative counterpart" to Booker T. Washington's idealism--"his acceptance of American culture and
his desire to be assimilated into it." Chesnutt and Dunbar
"avoided the tensions of the Negro mind" by creating dialect stories and poems similar to those of the white authors of the 1880's and 1890's.

8   HUGGINS, NATHAN IRVIN. <u>The Harlem Renaissance</u>. New York:
Oxford University Press, pp. 200, 232.
    Chesnutt is mentioned in a consideration of the cultural
and literary attitudes that bind the black writer. Questions whether he, and others, have had any choice other
than to reiterate "the message so often expressed in
American fiction, that the true American tragedy was to
be less than pure white."

9   JAMES, CHARLES L. "The Folk Tale Tradition," in <u>From the</u>
<u>Roots: Short Stories by Black Americans</u>. Edited by Charles
L. James. New York: Dodd, Mead and Co., pp. 4-5.
    An introduction to some of Chesnutt's short stories.
Chesnutt's "roots" are in the black folk tradition. "What
is significant about the folk tales of Charles Chesnutt is
that they are original stories, not merely adaptations of
old or well known tales."

10   McPHERSON, JAMES, et al. "Black Fiction at the Turn of the
Century: Charles Waddell Chesnutt and Paul Laurence
Dunbar," in <u>Blacks in America: Bibliographical Essays</u>.
Garden City, New York: Doubleday and Co., pp. 174-75.

Dunbar and Chesnutt are considered the two most important novelists at the turn of the century. Although The Marrow of Tradition is noteworthy, Chesnutt's best work was his short stories. Includes bibliographical essay.

11 MILLER, RUTH. Blackamerican Literature 1760–Present. Beverly Hills, California: Glencoe Press, pp. 286–87.
    A biographical and critical account introducing "The Wife of His Youth." Chesnutt's writing moved steadily in the direction of being more "serious" by prodding Americans to abandon caste distinction. As this protest sharpened, Chesnutt thought less and less of being judged for his craftsmanship.

12 REILLY, JOHN M. "The Dilemma in Chesnutt's The Marrow of Tradition." Phylon, 32 (First Quarter), pp. 31–38.
    Chesnutt "did much to establish irony as the predominant mode of perception in the universe of Negro fiction." Thorough analysis of The Marrow of Tradition, which represents Chesnutt's "mature style," is given. The conclusion of the novel is "unresolved," because "the novelist is in the dilemma of having so powerfully documented the corruption of white society that it is impossible to honor the ideal of integrating into it." Chesnutt must have felt this dilemma personally. The Colonel's Dream, and a late unpublished manuscript, further reveal Chesnutt's dilemma. "For all practical purposes . . . the irresolution apparent in The Marrow of Tradition and reinforced in The Colonel's Dream marks the end of Chesnutt's literary career."

13 SLOAN, IRVING J. Blacks in America 1492–1970: A Chronology and Fact Book. Dobbs Ferry, New York: Oceana Publications, pp. 16, 24, 29.
    Notes Chesnutt's birth, the publication of The House Behind the Cedars, and Chesnutt's reception of the Spingarn Medal.

14 STARKE, CATHERINE JUANITA. Black Portraiture in American Fiction: Stock Characters, Archetypes, and Individuals. New York: Basic Books, pp. 54, 56–59, 95–96, 98–99.
    The free slave as stock character is considered in "The Goophered Grapevine." The archetype of the tragic mulatto is viewed in "Her Virginia Mammy," "The Wife of His Youth," and in The House Behind the Cedars.

15 TRENT, TONI. "Stratification Among Blacks by Black Authors." Negro History Bulletin, 34 (December), 179–81.

An analysis of mulatto superiority in nineteenth century black fiction, relying primarily on the works of Chesnutt. Chesnutt was "so color-conscious that he reacted to the controls society placed upon him by completely alienating himself from the Black race and joining the white community." Stratification among blacks "is explainable in terms of white brainwashing."

1972 A BOOKS - NONE

1972 B SHORTER WRITINGS

1   ANDREWS, WILLIAM L. "Chesnutt's Patesville: The Presence and Influence of the Past in The House Behind the Cedars." College Language Association Journal, 15 (March), 284-94.
        The House Behind the Cedars is "an illustration of the social effects and moral consequences of a particular people's imperviousness to the passing of time and the changes which supposedly accompany it." Its theme is "the power of tradition to stymie beneficial change." Includes analysis of the novel.

2   BAKER, HOUSTON A., JR. Long Black Song: Essays on Black American Literature and Culture. Charlottesville, Virginia: University of Virginia Press, pp. 38-39, 136.
        Chesnutt was the first black American prose writer of distinction. The Conjure Woman draws upon black folk experience.

3   _____. "Balancing the Perspective, A Look at Early Black American Artistry," Negro American Literature Forum, 6 (Fall), 65-70.
        In a study of colonial and early nineteenth century black American writers, Chesnutt mentioned as a "conscious and accomplished craftsman" who was aware of his predecessors and influenced by them. "Dunbar and Chesnutt took the best of the black folk tradition and the best of the conscious literary tradition and produced works that sometimes reach greatness."

4   BARKSDALE, RICHARD and KENETH KINNAMON, eds. Black Writers of America: A Comprehensive Anthology. New York: The Macmillan Co., pp. 324-28.
        An introduction to a selection of Chesnutt's work, that includes a biographical sketch and a critical estimate. Chesnutt was "a careful literary artist, especially in the short story, whose craft as well as themes made him an

auspicious early master of Afro-American writing." Although most critics consider his short stories to be superior to his novels, "which are more polemical and less firmly constructed," his novels stand out: The House Behind the Cedars, The Marrow of Tradition, and The Colonel's Dream.

5   BRITT, DAVID D. "Chesnutt's Conjure Tales: What You See Is What You Get." College Language Association Journal, 15 (March), 269-83.
      "The Conjure Woman is primarily a study in duplicity that masks or reveals its meaning according to the predisposition of the reader." Includes an analysis of the stories.

6   BURKE, W. J., and WILL D. HOWE. American Authors and Books. New York: Crown Publishers, p. 115.
      A bibliography of Chesnutt's books and a reference to Helen M. Chesnutt's biography. See 1952.A1.

7   CHAMETZKY, JULES. "Our Decentralized Literature: A Consideration of Regional, Ethnic, Racial, and Sexual Factors." Jahrbuch für Amerikastudien, 17 (Winter), 56-72.
      The reputation that Chesnutt and some other writers, such as Cable, enjoyed at the turn of the century was based on their being classified as local color writers. This designation minimized their true concern which went to the heart of America's dilemmas: the racial grounds of the southern tragedy, the stakes involved in the acculturation of immigrant populations, and the assertion of a black ethos.

8   DAVIS, RUSSELL L. Black Americans in Cleveland: From George Peake to Carl B. Stokes 1796-1969. Washington, D. C.: The Associated Publishers, pp. 98, 117, 121, 150, 159, 194, 206-208, 222, 243, 245, 342.
      Chesnutt mentioned frequently as a prominent Cleveland citizen and writer. A biographical sketch is given, emphasizing his Cleveland connections.

9   EMERSON, O. B. "Cultural Nationalism in Afro-American Literature," in The Cry of Home: Cultural Nationalism and the Modern Writer. Edited by Ernest Lewald. Knoxville: University of Tennessee Press, pp. 211-44.
      Chesnutt mentioned as one of the few black writers who did not ignore black cultural expression before the Harlem Renaissance.

1972

10 GILES, JAMES R. "Chesnutt's Primus and Annie: A Contemporary
      View of The Conjure Woman." Markham Review, 3 (May), 46-49.
        The Conjure Woman is a "schizophrenic book" that presents
      both patronizingly stereotyped characters and honest pro-
      test. Too frequently the characters exhibit the worst black
      stereotypes. Julius and Primus are good examples of this.
      In order to cancel these influences, Annie, the employer of
      Julius, adds a dimension of protest.

11 HAYDN, HIRAM. "Charles W. Chesnutt." American Scholar, 42
      (Winter), 123-24.
        A brief account of an incident that occurred in the
      1920's when Chesnutt moved to Cleveland. Howell Haydn,
      professor of Biblical literature at Western Reserve Uni-
      versity, confronted the objections of Chesnutt's white
      neighbors when Chesnutt moved into the neighborhood.

12 HORNSBY, ALTON, JR. The Black Almanac. New York: Barron's
      Educational Series, p. 43.
        Between 1900 and 1905, Chesnutt "established himself as
      the foremost Afro-American novelist of his time." The
      Conjure Woman was his best work.

13 KENT, GEORGE E. Blackness and the Adventure of Western
      Culture. Chicago: Third World Press, pp. 12-13, 18, 185.
        Chesnutt is discussed in relation to both white and
      black American writing, and the complexities of his situa-
      tion novels are treated. Chesnutt was a precursor to the
      Harlem Renaissance.

14 _____. "Patterns of the Harlem Renaissance," in The Harlem
      Renaissance Remembered. Edited by Arna Bontemps. New York:
      Dodd, Mead and Co., pp. 22-34.
        Chesnutt was an important influence on the writers of
      the Harlem Renaissance. His work with black folk traditions
      was especially important. He accomplished a number of
      things: he produced "Baxter's Procrustes," "a short story
      that shows complete mastery of the form"; he made more use
      of "the folk's supernaturalist and conjure tradition in
      The Conjure Woman than has since been made of it"; and he
      made "an effective use of 'fooling massa' folk tradition."
      However, the Harlem writers would revolt from Chesnutt's
      use of the myths of whiteness in his novels, particularly
      his tendency to associate culture primarily with light-
      skinned characters.

15 LONG, RICHARD A., and EUGENIA W. COLLIER, eds. Afro-American
      Writing: An Anthology of Prose and Poetry. New York:
      New York University Press, pp. 115-16, 199-201.

Chesnutt was the most talented black writer at the turn of the century. Both his short stories and novels are treated in an introduction to one of his stories. His early folk stories, rooted in black folk material, often ironically reveal "the black face behind the white mask," while the stories published in The Wife of His Youth probe "the absurdity of the mulatto's position." Of Chesnutt's stories that do not deal with black people, "Baxter's Procrustes" is the best. His novels were not so successful as his short stories. Objectivity is lost in these, and the level is seldom above propaganda. The House Behind the Cedars is the best novel; the other two contain more anger than order.

16 SIMON, MYRON. Ethnic Writers in America. New York: Harcourt, Brace, Jovanovich, pp. 79-80.
    A biographical sketch introducing "The Wife of His Youth." Chesnutt wrote with the purpose of trying to overturn the color line.

17 SKAGGS, MERRILL MAGUIRE. The Folk of Southern Fiction. Athens, Georgia: University of Georgia Press, pp. 43, 58, 84, 97-99, 131.
    Chesnutt was a local color writer who used folk and local materials. Discusses "The Sheriff's Children" and "The Web of Circumstance."

18 TELLER, WALTER. "Charles W. Chesnutt's Conjuring and Color-Line Stories." American Scholar, 42 (Winter), 125-27.
    A brief account of Chesnutt's emergence as a writer, including an autobiographical sketch, Chesnutt's attitudes toward his efforts as a writer, and summary comment on his major works.

19 WIDEMAN, JOHN. "Charles W. Chesnutt: The Marrow of Tradition." American Scholar, 42 (Winter), 128-34.
    An analysis of The Marrow of Tradition, and consideration of the cultural and historical background against which it was written. It is a novel "that is subtle, complex, and suggestive far beyond the treatment traditionally accorded it."

20 WINTZ, CARY D. "Race and Realism in the Fiction of Charles W. Chesnutt." Ohio History, 81 (Spring), 122-30.
    Chesnutt's major significance "is that he was black, and that he was one of the first to successfully depict the condition of blacks in post-Civil War America." He was successful in a "basically hostile environment." Utilizes biographical information and analyzes major works.

1973

1973 A BOOKS

1 HOWSE, BETH M. Charles W. Chesnutt Collection. Nashville:
   Fisk University Library.
      An updated list of the papers and materials in the col-
   lection at Fisk University, Nashville, Tennessee. See
   1954.A1.

2 MEBANE, MARY ELIZABETH. "The Family in the Works of Charles
   W. Chesnutt and Selected Works of Richard Wright." Ph.D.
   dissertation, University of North Carolina.
      "In the works of Charles W. Chesnutt the structure of
   the black family clearly emerges in three stages: the
   slave family, the mulatto family, and the black bourgeois
   family." Since Chesnutt was a product of the latter family
   type, it becomes the ideal in his fiction.

1973 B SHORTER WRITINGS

1 APTHEKER, HERBERT. Annotated Bibliography of the Published
   Writings of W. E. B. DuBois. Millwood, New York: Kraus-
   Thomson Organization Ltd., pp. 17, 294, 300, 340, 443, 509,
   513, 543.
      Chesnutt mentioned occasionally by DuBois, in his pub-
   lished work.

2 _____, ed. The Correspondence of W. E. B. DuBois. Vol. 1.
   Amherst: University of Massachusetts Press, pp. 62, 378.
      Chesnutt's biography of Frederick Douglass is mentioned
   in a letter written by DuBois in 1903. In a letter to
   V. F. Calverton in 1928, DuBois responds to Calverton's
   request for assistance in assembling selections for Calver-
   ton's Anthology of American Negro Literature (1929). Du-
   Bois suggests that Chesnutt's short story, "The Wife of
   His Youth," is "one of the best short stories there is."
   See 1929.B4.

3 BASKIN, WADE, and RICHARD N. RUNES, eds. Dictionary of Black
   Culture. New York: Philosophical Library, pp. 89-90.
      A biographical sketch focused on Chesnutt's work as an
   attorney, educator, and writer. Some of his published books
   are noted.

4 CLARK, MARGARET GOFF. "Charles Waddell Chesnutt: Writer Who
   Chose to be Black," in Their Eyes on the Stars: Four Black
   Writers. Champaign, Illinois: Garrard Publishing Co.,
   pp. 127-69.

A book for younger readers. Includes a biographical
sketch. Chesnutt's life was exemplary and his decision not
to pass for white, but to inspire other blacks with his example, is notable. His writing career was short, but
"brilliant." "He is considered the most competent black
writer of fiction before the 1920's. His work proved that
writing ability had nothing to do with race or skin color."

5 FLEMING, ROBERT E. "Black, White, and Mulatto in Martin R.
     Delaney's [sic] Blake." Negro History Bulletin, 36
     (February), 37-39.
        Unlike Martin R. Delany, Chesnutt is an example of a
     black writer whose works "imply that mulattoes and quadroons
     are actually superior to black people."

6 _____. "Humor in the Early Black Novel." College Language
     Association Journal, 17 (December), 250-62.
        Chesnutt "is probably the most sophisticated black novel-
     ist of the period, [and] his use of comedy to cut down the
     pompous white is less physical and more subtle than the
     methods of such writers as Griggs and Webb." Comments on
     Major McLean in The Colonel's Dream.

7 HARRIS, TRUDIER. "The Tie That Binds: The Function of Folk-
     lore in the Fiction of Charles Waddell Chesnutt, Jean
     Toomer, and Ralph Ellison." Ph.D. dissertation, Ohio State
     University.
        A study of the structural and thematic uses of folklore
     in works of the three. Examines The Conjure Woman. Ches-
     nutt's use of folk material is accurate to the oral tradi-
     tion. He views black folk culture as a means of showing
     his white reading audience that blacks are not the ignorant,
     superstitious stereotypes whites often assume them to be.
     Thus Chesnutt censors his characters who actively show kin-
     ship to folk materials. He feels that blacks should re-
     place their unscientific folk culture with education, and
     thus pave the way for their assimilation into the dominant
     culture.

8 HOVIT, THEODORE R. "Chesnutt's 'The Goophered Grapevine' as
     Social Criticism." Negro American Literature Forum, 7
     (Fall), 86-88.
        This story is "primarily concerned with deep and funda-
     mental problems in American society." Its point is made
     by interrelating two narrative viewpoints--that of the
     northern entrepreneur and Julius, an ex-slave. It can be
     read as a "parable which explains the consequences of an
     unbounded faith in economic progress and the way such be-
     lief serves to conceal the cost in human dignity."

9   RUBIN, LOUIS D., JR. <u>The Comic Tradition in American Litera-
      ture</u>. New Brunswick, New Jersey: Rutgers University Press,
      pp. 352, 359.
          Chesnutt was a writer who drew many of his short story
      plots from black folk literature. "The Passing of Grandi-
      son" is told with "disciplined narrative control and sus-
      pense. The net effect of the story is comic in the best
      sense of the word."

10   SCHRAUFNAGEL, NOEL. <u>From Apology to Protest: The Black
      American Novel</u>. Deland, Florida: Everett/Edwards, pp. 8-9.
          Chesnutt "sounded the note of racial protest, still
      basically apologetic, that dominated black fiction early
      in the twentieth century." <u>The House Behind the Cedars</u> is
      the best of his three novels. "Chesnutt's fiction suffers
      as a result of his propagandistic purposes."

11   SHEPARD, RAY ANTHONY. Introduction, in <u>Conjure Tales by
      Charles W. Chesnutt as Retold by Ray Anthony Shepard</u>.
      New York: E. P. Dutton and Co., pp. vii-ix.
          A biographical and critical introduction to tales by
      Chesnutt, retold for the younger reader. Discusses the
      meaning of "conjuring," and compares Chesnutt's work to
      that of Joel Chandler Harris.

12   WALCOTT, RONALD. "Chesnutt's 'The Sheriff's Children' as
      Parable." <u>Negro American Literature Forum</u>, 7 (Fall),
      83-85.
          "'The Sheriff's Children' is a parable of the Recon-
      struction South, with a biblical parallel." The sheriff
      represents the southern white to whom Chesnutt addressed
      his stories, the liberal element who was interested in
      social change but who was "committed to the very historical
      attitudes and institutions which, by their very nature,
      make change impossible." The relationship between the
      sheriff's son, a mulatto, and his half sister, a white
      girl, is "very much like that of Cain and Abel."

13   WHITLOW, ROGER. <u>Black American Literature: A Critical
      History</u>. Chicago: Nelson Hall, pp. 11, 54, 60-64, 95,
      219.
          Primarily a biographical sketch and a critical consider-
      ation of Chesnutt's books. Robert Farnsworth's introduc-
      tion to the 1969 reprinting of <u>The Conjure Woman</u> is quoted
      to show that this book "illustrates the terms under which
      the white American reading public . . . was willing to let
      an Afro-American put his foot on the ladder of literary
      success." Both this volume, and the next, reveal rich

prose and an excellent sense of dialect. The novels of
Chesnutt display all the nineteenth century conventions--
"two dimensional characters, coincidence in abundance,
melodramatically mistreated heroines"--but they are worth
reading. A bibliographical section devoted to fiction by
American blacks includes a list of Chesnutt's books. See
1969.B3.

1974 A BOOKS

1   ANDREWS, WILLIAM LEAKE. "The Fiction of Charles W. Chesnutt."
        Ph.D. dissertation, University of North Carolina.
            Chesnutt's short stories were by far more successful
        than his novels. The stories modify many of the popular
        literary stereotypes regarding black characters and intro-
        duce new aspects to the character of the black figure.
        They employ satire, irony, and a realism that occasionally
        borders on naturalism. The novels are uneven. They are
        occasionally fiercely partisan, and employ stereotyped
        characters and situations in sometimes technically flawed
        ways.

2   CUNNINGHAM, DOROTHY JOAN. "The Published Fiction of Charles
        Waddell Chesnutt: A Critical Analysis." Ph.D. disserta-
        tion, Florida State University.
            An analytical study of the fiction. "Each selection is
        analyzed on the basis of plot, character development,
        setting, theme, language, style, and technique."

3   HEERMANCE, J. NOEL. Charles W. Chesnutt: America's First
        Great Black Novelist. Hamden, Connecticut: The Shoe
        String Press, 258 pp.
            A biography that attempts "to view Chesnutt's artistic
        greatness within the context of his total environment."
        Considers the cultural, historical, and literary back-
        grounds affecting Chesnutt. His "basic nature" was af-
        fected by middle class values, intellectual and racial iso-
        lation, and a concern with social inequities. Speculates
        as to why Chesnutt wrote and then ceased writing. Dis-
        cusses his art in terms of themes, techniques, and purposes.
        Bibliography included.

4   TERRY, EUGENE. "A Critical Analysis of Charles Waddell
        Chesnutt's The Conjure Woman and The Wife of His Youth and
        Other Stories of the Color Line." Ph.D. dissertation,
        University of Massachusetts.

1974

   Considers the sixteen stories in two books by Chesnutt.
Attempts to show that Chesnutt's work is more than that of
a "second-rate local colorist," an attitude often taken by
white critics, or more than that of a writer with little
concern for the plight of American blacks, a charge often
made by black readers.

1974 B SHORTER WRITINGS

1 BELL, BERNARD W. "Literary Sources of the Early Afro-American
  Novel." College Language Association Journal, 18
  (September), 29-43.
   "The primary unifying metaphor in the Afro-American
  novel is the quest for identity as free men." This is an
  "archtypal journey, usually cast in a Christian framework."
  In The Marrow of Tradition, "The Promised Land" is the
  south.

2 CHANDONIA, RONALD PAUL. "The New South in Black and White:
  Afro-American Fiction From the End of Reconstruction Until
  the First World War." Ph.D. dissertation, Emory University.
   Chesnutt was a major writer who helped "inaugurate the
  Afro-American tradition in American fiction." Chesnutt
  castigated southern values in his work, both indirectly
  and overtly.

3 DAVIS, ARTHUR P. From the Dark Tower: Afro-American Writers
  1900-1960. Washington, D. C.: Howard University Press,
  pp. 6, 30, 65.
   Chesnutt and Paul Laurence Dunbar were successful and
  distinguished writers who wrote primarily before the twentieth century. Dunbar was largely an accommodationist,
  but Chesnutt was largely a militant. Their success spurred
  all black writers and their use of folk material gave the
  writers of the Harlem Renaissance a precedent. With his
  stories of protest and passing, Chesnutt set the stage for
  much that was to come.

4 DIXON, MELVIN. "The Teller as Folk Trickster in Chesnutt's
  The Conjure Woman." College Language Association Journal,
  18 (December), 186-97.
   The Conjure Woman is "a folk novel that describes a
  series of adventures of equal importance." The "progres-
  sion" in the character of the teller, Julius, provides
  "the unity of the novel."

5   HEMENWAY, ROBERT. "'Baxter's Procrustes': Irony and Pro-
      test." College Language Association Journal, 18 (December),
      172-85.
          Chesnutt's story is probably a protest "directed towards
      a specific act of discrimination: the refusal of the
      Rowfant Club, a Cleveland literary society, to grant Ches-
      nutt membership." Considers historical evidence for this
      view, and includes full interpretation of the story.

6   RENDER, SYLVIA L., ed. "Introduction," in The Short Fiction
      of Charles W. Chesnutt. Washington, D. C.: Howard Uni-
      versity Press, pp. 3-56.
          A biographical and extended critical consideration that
      includes discussion of all of Chesnutt's short fiction,
      whether included in the volume or not. Views Chesnutt's
      life in the south and the north. Notes the public recep-
      tion of his writing. Studies local color, characteriza-
      tion, point of view, tone, humor, satire, irony, theme and
      general style in Chesnutt's short fiction.

7   ROSENBLATT, ROGER. Black Fiction. Cambridge: Harvard
      University Press, pp. 7, 82, 170.
          If the slave narratives, which are not properly works
      of fiction, are omitted, the only black fiction of signi-
      ficance in America is modern fiction, with the exception
      of works by Chesnutt, Frank Webb, Martin Delany, and
      William Wells Brown.

8   SMITH, DWIGHT L., ed. Afro-American History: A Bibliography.
      Santa Barbara, California: Clio Press, pp. 42, 58, 469.
          Cites three secondary articles by Julian D. Mason, John
      Henrik Clarke, and José Gonzáles. See 1966.B4; 1967.B2;
      1968.B3.

9   SPILLER, ROBERT E., et al. Literary History of the United
      States: Bibliography. Fourth edition. New York:
      Macmillan Publishing Co., p. 440.
          A list of books by Chesnutt, and a bibliographic essay
      focusing on secondary sources.

1975 A   BOOKS

1   GECAU, JAMES KIMANI. "Charles W. Chesnutt and His Literary
      Crusade." Ph.D. dissertation, State University of New
      York at Buffalo.
          Chesnutt was a "pioneer of twentieth century Afro-
      American fiction." His writing was directed against the

negative black stereotypes popularized by the plantation
tradition, and particularly in his first work, assumed an
ironic tone. His later works focused on near-white characters, aspiring toward middle class respectability. Though
he satirized these, he was sympathetic to their aspirations
and ambivalent toward "pure" blacks who were farthest from
the possibilities of racial assimilation. His last works
took a closer look at the white world into which he had
hoped to assimilate his characters, and found it debased.
Unable to justify his characters' wish to be assimilated,
he continued to hope for a harmonious society attainable
through assimilation. By the end of his writing career,
Chesnutt had grown pessimistic. He realized he could not
re-educate an audience that continued to want old negative
stereotypes.

1975 B SHORTER WRITINGS

1   BONE, ROBERT. Down Home: A History of Afro-American Short
     Fiction From its Beginnings to the End of the Harlem
     Renaissance. New York: G. P. Putnam's Sons, pp. xiii, xv,
     xix, 5-7, 8, 11-12, 17-18, 22, 23, 26, 28, 44, 51, 52, 55,
     74-105, 109, 112, 139.
         A bibliographical and critical consideration of Ches-
     nutt's short fiction. Chesnutt was "a literary artist of
     first rank" and "a major American writer." Chesnutt re-
     fused the traditions of the plantation school and struck
     at the heart of the southern pastoral. His art is rooted
     in antithesis and opposition, and, drawing on the satiri-
     cal sources of black folklore, founds a tradition that
     descends through Langston Hughes to Ishmael Reed. Ches-
     nutt's two books of short stories, and a few uncollected
     short tales, are examined. The Conjure Woman is Chesnutt's
     chief work in which the literary form made popular by Joel
     Chandler Harris is infused with a new and subversive con-
     tent. The Wife of His Youth has fewer major stories than
     Chesnutt's first book. It lacks a unity of design and is
     marred by sentimentality.

2   BOSWELL, J. C. "A Black Grimm." New Republic, 172 (1 March),
     31.
         Review of The Short Fiction of Charles W. Chesnutt,
     edited by Sylvia Lyons Render. Chesnutt is a "vastly
     underrated" writer, and his "eclipse" by Twain, Crane,
     Howells, and James is "unconscionable." "His specialty is
     the dramatic presentation of subtle characters against
     authentic backgrounds." Includes a brief biography.
     See 1974.B6.

Charles W. Chesnutt: A Reference Guide

3   GAYLE, ADDISON. The Way of the New World: The Black Novel in America. Garden City, New York: Doubleday, pp. 5, 12, 47-58, 62, 67, 74.

Chesnutt's writing is compared to that of Dunbar, Washington, and others. The major objective of Chesnutt's fiction "is to plead the case of the mulatto before his white audience, to seek not so much to create new images but to counteract those prevalent in the literature of the day." The House Behind the Cedars and The Marrow of Tradition are considered in detail. The former is his best effort in long fiction.

4   MATTHEWS, GERALDINE O., and the African-American Materials Project Staff. Black American Writers 1773-1949: A Bibliography and Union List. Boston: G. K. Hall and Co., p. 132.

A list of writings by Chesnutt in the libraries of six southeastern states: Alabama, Georgia, North Carolina, South Carolina, Tennessee, and Virginia.

5   RUSH, THERESSA G., CAROL F. MYERS, and ESTHER S. ARATA. Black American Writers Past and Present: A Biographical and Bibliographical Dictionary. Vol. 1. Metuchen, New Jersey: Scarecrow Press, pp. 142-49.

A biographical sketch and a list of primary and secondary materials.

6   TURNER, ARLIN. "Dim Pages in Literary History: The South Since the Civil War," in Southern Literary Study: Problems and Possibilities. Edited by Louis D. Rubin, Jr., and C. Hugh Holman. Chapel Hill: University of North Carolina Press, pp. 43, 46.

Discussion of "problems of interpretation and assessment" in southern literature. "The career of Charles W. Chesnutt is especially useful . . . for the light it throws on the racial aspects of authorship in the decades following the Civil War." For Chesnutt, "characters of the two races presented separate but inseparable problems. Back of him, few members of his race had written stories or novels dealing with either race." Like other writers, Chesnutt "could not forget that he was a southerner." "No Negro author in the South then--or today perhaps--could escape multiplied and disturbing forces on his pen."

Index

INDEX

Pittsburg *Gazette, The Colonel's Dream,* 1905.B66

Pittsburg *Post, The House Behind the Cedars,* 1900.B85

Pittsburg *Times, Frederick Douglass,* 1899.B122

plantation tradition, 1899.B28, B45, B61-62, B64, B74, B109, B114; 1900.B102; 1905.B29; 1924.B3; 1934.B1; 1941.B2; 1948.B5; 1949.B4; 1956.B1; 1963.B5; 1966.B8; 1969.B3; 1970.B9, B16; 1975.A1, B1

Ploski, Harry A., 1967.B3

Portland (Maine) *Advertiser, The Marrow of Tradition,* 1901.B33; *The Wife of His Youth,* 1899.B103

Portland (Maine) *Transcript, The Conjure Woman,* 1899.B20; *Frederick Douglass,* 1900.B7

Portland (Oregon) *Oregonian, The House Behind the Cedars,* 1901.B14; *The Marrow of Tradition,* 1901.B30

"Po' Sandy," 1899.B51, B71

"Postscript: Chesnutt," 1933.B3

Primus, 1972.B10

Proceedings of Conference of College Teachers of English of Texas, 1970.B2

Progress of a Race, 1902.B21

Providence (Rhode Island) *Journal, Frederick Douglass,* 1899.B116; *The House Behind the Cedars,* 1900.B66

"Psychological Counter-Current in Recent Fiction, A," 1901.B59

"Published Fiction of Charles Waddell Chesnutt: A Critical Analysis, The," 1974.A2

Publisher's Weekly, 1932.B2; 1937.B4

Quarles, Benjamin, 1964.B3

Quest for Equality, The, 1968.B14

Quinn, Arthur Hobson, 1951.B1

Race Consciousness and the American Negro, 1934.B1

Race Problem, The, 1903.B1

"Race and Realism in the Fiction of Charles W. Chesnutt," 1972.B20

race relations, 1899.B52, B61, B80, B87, B91, B97, B102, B110-13, B115, B124, B127; 1900.B2-3, B12, B14, B18-20, B23-24, B29-31, B36, B55, B62, B64, B67, B79, B82-83, B85, B89, B90-91, B93, B99; 1901.B5, B9, B11, B24, B29, B31, B35, B37, B41, B45, B47, B55, B58-59; 1902.B1-4, B10-11, B13, B15, B17; 1903.B1; 1905.B3, B14-16, B18, B20-21, B25, B33, B37-38, B45, B47, B49, B63; 1910.B3; 1926.B1; 1933.B3; 1934.B2; 1939.B1; 1941.B2; 1942.B2; 1948.B1; 1952.B4; 1953.B3; 1958.B3, B5; 1959.B2-3; 1962.A1, B1; 1963.B4; 1966.B6, B10, B12; 1968.B8-9; 1969.B5, B9; 1970.B16; 1972.B16

Race Relations, 1934.B2; *The House Behind the Cedars*

Raleigh (North Carolina) *News and Observer, The Conjure Woman,* 1899.B47

Reade, Charles, 1905.B28

Reader's Encyclopedia, The, 1948.B1

Reader's Encyclopedia of American Literature, The, 1962.B4

realism, 1900.B64, B66; 1901.B4, B13, B37; 1905.B7; 1924.B1; 1953.B1; 1956.B1; 1959.B2; 1962.B1; 1968.B10; 1969.B4-5; 1970.B8; 1971.B2; 1974.A1

Realist at War: The Mature Years 1885-1920 of William Dean Howells, The, 1958.B2

Redding, J. Saunders, 1939.B2; 1949.B4; 1950.B4-5; 1958.B4; 1964.B4; 1971.B5

Reed, Ishmael, 1975.B1

INDEX

INDEX

"Two New Novelists," 1900.B105

Uncle Tom's Cabin, 1901.B22-23,
    B25-26, B33, B36, B46, B57;
    1902.B5, B12, B15, B19;
    1905.B41-42
"Uncle Wellington's Wives,"
    1900.B101
Up From Slavery, 1902.B16
Utica (New York) Observer, The
    Colonel's Dream, 1905.B58

Van Deusen, John G., 1944.B1
Van Vechten, Carl, 1925.B2;
    1927.B3
Virginia, 1905.B8
Voice of the Negro, 1905.B65;
    The Colonel's Dream, 1906.B4

Walcott, Ronald, 1973.B12
Walden, Rena, 1900.B55, B59-60,
    B63, B65, B73, B78, B91;
    1901.B1, B3, B6; 1938.B1
Walls Came Tumbling Down, The,
    1970.B12
Warwick, John, 1900.B55, B59,
    B69; 1901.B6; 1938.B1
Walser, Richard, 1948.B6;
    1970.B15
Washington, Booker T., 1899.B93,
    B105; 1900.B6, B15, B36,
    B76; 1902.B15-16; 1909.B1;
    1913.B1; 1962.B1;
    1963.B4; 1969.B5, B10;
    1970.B5; 1971.B7; 1975.B3
Washington, D. C. Daily Record,
    1899.B89; The Conjure Woman,
    1899.B53
Washington, D. C. Evening Star,
    The Marrow of Tradition,
    1901.B29
Washington, D. C. Star, The
    Colonel's Dream, 1905.B11
Washington, D. C. Times, The
    Conjure Woman, 1899.B28;
    Frederick Douglass, 1899.B112;
    "The Future American,"
    1900.B53; The House Behind
    the Cedars, 1900.B67; The
    Wife of His Youth, 1900.B4

Way of the New World, The,
    1975.B3; The House Behind
    the Cedars, The Marrow of
    Tradition
Weatherford, Willis D., 1924.B4;
    1934.B2
"Web of Circumstance, The,"
    1899.B119; 1972.B17
Webb, Frank, 1973.B6; 1974.B7
Wellman, Mary Wade, 1965.B5
Wesley, Charles H., 1928.B8;
    1968.B14
"What Is a White Man?," 1899.B79
"White Stereotypes in Fiction
    by Negroes," 1950.B2
Whiteman, Maxwell, 1955.B3
Wideman, John, 1972.B19
"Wife of His Youth, The,"
    1898.B1-3, B5-6, B8; 1899.B1,
    B4-5, B101, B113, B119;
    1900.B28, B101; 1910.B1-2;
    1937.B1; 1971.B14
Wife of His Youth, The, 1899.B85,
    B91-94, B98, B100-106,
    B108-111, B113-115, B118-119,
    B123; 1900.B1, B3-5, B9,
    B11-15, B20, B22-26, B28-34,
    B39-40, B42, B45-47, B49,
    B80, B88, B101, B104-105;
    1901.B56, B61; 1905.B8;
    1906.B1; 1910.B1-2; 1916.B1;
    1937.B3; 1941.B2; 1948.B4;
    1959.B1; 1968.B10, B13;
    1970.B3, B6; 1971.B6;
    1972.B15; 1973.B2; 1974.A4;
    1975.B1
Williams, George W., 1968.B2
Williams, Kenny J., 1970.B16
Wilmington (North Carolina)
    Messenger, "The Bouquet,"
    1900.B19; The Marrow of
    Tradition, 1902.B3
Wilmington, North Carolina, riot,
    1901.B36; 1902.B3; 1909.B1;
    1921.B1; 1967.B1; 1969.B7
Winkelman, Donald M., 1965.B5
Wintz, Cary D., 1972.B20
witchcraft, 1899.B28, B35,
    B38-39, B49, B58, B64-66,
    B72, B78
Witlow, Roger, 1973.B13

149

INDEX

Woodson, Carter G., 1928.B8;
   1930.B1
Woodward, C. Vann, 1966.B12
Worcester (Massachusetts) *Spy,*
   The Conjure Woman, 1899.B42;
   The House Behind the Cedars,
   1900.B71; *The Marrow of*
   Tradition, 1901.B52
Work, Monroe Nathan, 1928.B9
Wright, John Livingston, 1901.B61

Wright, Lyle H., 1966.B13
Wright, Richard, 1948.B3;
   1960.B1; 1968.B10; 1970.B2;
   1971.B5; 1973.A2
Writer, The, 1898.B4

Yorkshire (England) *Observer,*
   The Colonel's Dream,
   1905.B61